HIRE ME, INC.

ALSO AVAILABLE IN THE HIRE ME, INC. SERIES ...

Hire Me, Inc. Interviews

Hire Me, Inc. Package Yourself to Get Your Dream Job

For more information visit www.entrepreneurpress.com

Hire Me, Inc.

Resumes and Cover Letters

That Get Results

Roy J. Blitzer

EP
Entrepreneur®
Press

Editorial director: Jere L. Calmes
Cover design: Beth Hansen-Winter
Composition and production: CWL Publishing Enterprises, Inc., Madison, WI,
www.cwlpub.com

This publication is designed to provide accurate and authoritative information in regard to the
subject matter covered. It is sold with the understanding that the publisher is not engaged in
rendering legal, accounting, or other professional services. If legal advice or other expert assistance is required, the services of a competent professional person should be sought.

ISBN 13: 978-1-59918-083-0
       10: 1-59918-083-9

Library of Congress Cataloging-in-Publication Data

Blitzer, Roy J.
  Hire Me, Inc. resumes and cover letters : that get results / by Roy J. Blitzer.
    p. cm.
  ISBN-13: 978-1-59918-083-0 (alk. paper)
  ISBN-10: 1-59918-083-9 (alk. paper)
   1. Resumes (Employment)—Handbooks, manuals, etc. 2. Cover letters—Handbooks,
manuals, etc. 3. Applications for positions—Handbooks, manuals, etc. I. Title.
  HF5383.B527 2007
  650.14'2—dc22

                                                          2007008334

CONTENTS

ACKNOWLEDGMENTS

"Rome wasn't built in day."

Neither is your resume ... and neither is a book about how to construct one. Creating this text—about such a key ingredient for finding a satisfying job or for searching for a fulfilling career—required the energy, time, and expertise of a great many wonderful people.

I'd first like to thank my colleagues in the career counseling profession—friends and co-workers who worked side-by-side with me providing career counseling and outplacement services through the years—first at Syntex Corporation (now Roche Pharmaceuticals–F. Hoffman–LaRoche Ltd.), then at de Recat/Interim/Spherion and now at TMS, Torchiana, Mastrov and Sapiro (especially Al, Anna, Anne, Beth, Bert, Bill, Cathy, Cheryl, Connie, Dave, Eileen, Enid, Eve, Gary, Gene, Helen, Holly, Jack, Janet, Kathy, Kristi, Laura, Lido, Margot, Marlys, Maryann, Mary, Maureen, Megan, Mike, Pat, Steve, Sue, Susan, and Susie). You have been unselfish in sharing your experiences, previously created notes and written manuals/materials, and "what-works" tips of the trade. All have been lovingly massaged and painstakingly altered, and as part of the content of this book, will now continue to help a whole new set of people. I am forever grateful and appreciative to you and your professionalism.

All of the staff at Entrepreneur Media, my editor Karen Thomas in particular (and Jere Calmes and CWL Publishing Enterprises in the background) deserve recognition for their patience and understanding (of my limited—but constantly improving—word-processing and computer skills, especially). I also thank my agent, Jeff Herman, of the Jeff Herman Agency, whose support and recognition of my skills made this entire series a reality.

Special kudos to Matt Jones, whose editing and writing skills substantially enhanced the samples (and text) and whose first-hand knowledge of the resume-building process was invaluable to the flow of the content.

And finally, thanks to my immediate family: my wife Carol, a seasoned journalist and the legitimate writer in our group, for her support—and huge chunks of time—in final writing, proofing, and editing, and our daughters, Mara and Hannah, for their willingness to heed the advice and to craft resumes that got results and helped launch their professional lives so successfully and admirably.

INTRODUCTION

Creating Tools That Distinguish You and Make a Difference

W elome to *HIRE ME, Inc.: Resumes and Cover Letters That Get Results*, a comprehensive how-to plan for building your resume (and accompanying cover letter), perhaps the most important marketing tools for your career search and job satisfaction.

The aim of the complete HIRE ME, Inc. series is to present yourself as a product, a unique item being launched into the work marketplace. The goal of this book is to help you create the best marketing literature ever—the sales document and accompanying cover letter—that will present you in the most positive light and position you to get the best job possible. Your resume will help you launch this one-of-a-kind resource and create the opportunity for you to sell yourself in a personal interview.

The mantra for the world of real estate is location, location, location. The mantra for getting a job or finding the perfect career (see *HIRE ME, Inc.: Package Yourself to Get Your Dream Job*) is networking, networking, networking; the mantra for a successful interview (see *Interviews That Get Offers*) is preparation, preparation, preparation. The mantra here is results, results, results.

This is just as much a "do" book as it is a "read" book. For you to get the full benefit, you need to complete the exercise, fill in the blank, and experiment with options. To help you, you'll find a series of ROIs (Recommendations, Opinions, and Insights) throughout the book that provide either summarized or additional tips for your enrichment. Here's an example:

> ## ROI (Recommendations, Opinions, and Insights)
>
> Knowing the ingredients of the traditional Marketing Mix will help you develop a consistency in your approach. Seeing your resume as the key ingredient of your promotion plan can help distinguish you from the crowd.
>
> Product – You and what value you can bring to the organization
>
> Price – How much are you worth and what offer are you willing to accept?
>
> Place – Where are you willing to live, how much time are you willing to commute?
>
> Promotion – How are you going to present yourself and let people know you are not only available but the "perfect" fit?

There are also FTEs (Facts, Thoughts, and Examples) interspersed throughout to highlight key points and strengthen a recommendation or idea.

Keep your wits about you and your sense of humor intact as you start this exciting process. If you're ready, let's begin.

FTE (Facts, Thoughts, and Examples)

Keep two or three copies of your resume in each vehicle you own – carry supplies in a folio if you use public transportation and be prepared to distribute them. There are very few inappropriate times, and you should always strive for elegance in your font, paper bond, and color.

Dedication

This book is dedicated to those people whom I may have helped in some way to discover their passion and to earn their livelihoods in jobs and careers they love.

My hope is that they will bring inspiration to those still searching, and the future workplace will be filled with happy and productive individuals. The journey for job/career satisfaction is well worth the effort—your joy at doing what you're good at, what you love, and what's important to you can make that long-term difference.

THE CHOICES TO MAKE

Creating Tools That Distinguish You and Make a Difference

Perhaps your most valuable marketing tool is your resume. Your resume is often the first means hiring managers have to judge you. It alone does not get you the job, of course. The main goal of a powerful resume is to get you an interview and/or to move you forward in the search process.

The resume provides the summary you need to sell yourself and to highlight your background and accomplishments to the hiring team. It also serves as a roadmap the interviewer can use to craft questions that test your skills, knowledge, and value-fit for the job.

Your resume needs to generate a compelling marketing message at a glance on just a page or two. The average time for a resume review is merely 25 seconds. In our fast-paced, information-overload times, when everyone is accustomed to getting just the gist, the high-speed download, or the instant highlight, a hiring manager won't read your resume unless intrigued by a catchy presentation. It should play up your strengths and it should present results and accomplishments that address the needs of the marketplace.

Your resume needs to appeal to a variety of "buyers." The first is the hiring manager, someone who is looking for an ideal candidate fit. This sales tool needs to maximize your marketability for both his or her present and future needs, and is the key piece of literature, ad, or commercial that drives the recipient to check out the product first-hand, in person.

The HR representative must also see you as someone who will fit comfortably into the organization.

Your references read your resume as a refresher statement, a way for them to recall your unique accomplishments or to see where you have succeeded since you last worked.

Your network partners read your resume to help you validate your job goals and real successes.

Employment agency staff and recruiters scan your resume to standardize their candidate presentations; and in general, it is the best way to screen applicants not meeting their qualifications.

Remember: While many who read your resume may draw individual conclusions about your career, your resume needs to reflect the criteria that you believe make your work special and valuable to many employers.

Our society puts lots of emphasis on appearance. Your "look" during the job/career search process and the literature you create, however, has much more impact than a superficial impression—it states your personal image. You want to be sure that your brand image—and the packaging materials you generate to sell yourself—has a purpose, and shares your primary message for your buyer. It is a significant part of the mix.

Today, consumers evaluate many aspects of the total product offering, and packaging is a key part of any assessment. Companies now use packaging to change and improve their product offerings. Take the following, for example: a squeezable ketchup bottle that sits upside down on its cap for easy pouring, a salt container that ensures a uniform flow in all weather conditions, a square paint can with screw tops and built-in handles, a toothpaste tube that pumps, packaged popcorn and other microwavable food products, plastic oil can bottles with tops that eliminate the funnel. In each of these examples, the product package told the consumer the product was new and improved and this opened larger market segments for the items. What can you do to generate this kind of improved packaging and function in your product, yourself (without, of course, being able to "leap tall buildings in a single bound")?

Packaging can also make the offering more attractive to retailers, especially the Universal Product Codes and accompanying bar codes that provide valuable information on price, color, size, and sales volume. (With the new RFD chip, products can be tracked at all times and provide even more key data on visibility, attractiveness, and usefulness.)

Items that were once sold by a sales force are now available online or at self-serve outlets, so packaging has an even more compelling role. New laws make content and safety issues more important, too, and you now get more information than ever before.

Today, a product package must:

- Attract positive attention
- Describe the contents and present information
- Explain the benefits
- Provide warranty and guarantee data
- Give some price, use, and value facts
- Protect the contents from damage, theft, etc.

Some companies even package their services: Consider the Enterprise car pickup, Virgin Atlantic Airways door-to-door limousine option, and the financial institution that includes counsel on insurance or mutual fund purchase. (Caution: Make sure the additional service doesn't inflate the price. In your job offer "service package" don't hide your real salary requirements from a prospective employer.)

Your job in this process, no matter your desired field or position, is to broadcast an image of confidence and competence—in both your personal look and the sales materials (resume, bio, brochure, business card, and more). You want everyone you encounter to see that you can perform the work required, and that you are the person you appear to be … on paper and in person. (If you don't believe this, just think of poor Mr. Brown, who misrepresented himself in accepting the head position of FEMA and was disgraced before the entire nation during the Katrina disaster.)

FTE (Facts, Thoughts, and Examples)

A two-page resume is just fine, nowadays, especially for someone who has been in the workforce for many years. Be sure your second page has your name on it (Blitzer, page 2) … and … a paperclip might be the best way to keep them together, if the next step is a scanner and someone needs to quickly separate them.

VISUAL APPEARANCE

Your resume page(s) appearance (its design and verbal organization) is almost as important as its content. This package must be distinctive but not outlandish, inclusive but not confessional (save the latter for your partner or clergy). Unless you're in the creative fields or are a huge risk-taker, avoid shocking pink paper, pictures, and fanciful punctuation (especially exclamation marks!). None of these tricks will enhance your message and could easily backfire for a more serious hiring manager. One exception: a sports reporter who sent his resume to the newspaper editor inked on a basketball. OK, it was clever and marginally appropriate to the role, and he got the job, but you should generally restrict your distinctive resume presentation to perhaps placing it in an extra-large envelope that stands out.

FORMAT—STRUCTURE AND STYLE

Before you begin building the content of your resume, you need to decide which type and format are best for you. With the increasing use of technology, you need to be mindful of how your resume is really used. Human resource professionals and hiring managers still read and screen paperwork manually, but most organizations capture the contents of your resume electronically, using computer keyword-searching techniques. You need a resume, then, that is both attractive and sales-focused. It also should be in hard copy/presentation format, easy to scan, and computer-friendly.

FORMAT #1: SKILLS OR FUNCTIONAL RESUME

This format leads with emphasis on your successful experiences and abilities, with the organizations and summary/chronology—your job history and positions—listed at the end. It focuses on the special skills you've aquired and the results you've achieved vs. how, when, or where you acquired those skills and achieved those results. It emphasizes your unique contributions and strengths vs. your title, company, and time frame. This resume style can be an especially powerful tool when:

- You are changing fields or switching industries and de-emphasizing credentials.
- You are a seasoned professional with an extensive number of assignments and expertise.
- You are just entering the workforce and lack a time-line history of work.
- Your career has slumped and you want to revitalize it by focusing on your skill set.
- You are entering the civilian workforce after a career in the military.
- You are a "resumer"—returning to the workforce after an absence of many years.
- You are close to the end of your career and considering alternative options of employment.

Be advised that you may need to use this resume format selectively. You need to be aware that it can be seen in a way you may not intend. Some hiring managers and HR professionals discriminate against this skills-only focus. It raises a red flag for them, either signaling a non-linear, checkerboard career or telegraphing you are hiding something or not telling the real story. (What were you really doing the years not accounted for?)

If, however, the search is for someone who has a variety of experiences, is able to draw on a wealth of different backgrounds, or has the ability to reinvent himself or herself appropriately, it could be your ideal sales/marketing tool.

Sample #1: **Skills or Functional Resume**

STAR PERFORMANCE, CHA, CFE   e-mail: winner@hotstuff.com
549 Spotlight Avenue   Home (707) 555-3546
Oscar, CA 94510   Office (925) 555-4428

SUMMARY OF EXPERIENCE

International and domestic bank management experience including auditing, private banking, retail/consumer operations and wholesale compliance. Has demonstrated skills in strategic planning, foreign and domestic acquisitions, corporate restructuring, process flow improvements, premises optimization, and organizational effectiveness. Proven leadership in building teams and personnel management. Trilingual—English, Spanish, and Portuguese.

HIGHLIGHTS OF ACCOMPLISHMENTS

STRATEGIC PLANNING
- Planned and established strategic administrative and support offices in Panama, Colombia, Argentina, and Brazil.
- Downsized and restructured operations in Argentina, Brazil, and Mexico. Strategically organized compliance and operational support service units for the Global Private Bank, Latin America, Europe, and Asia.

MANAGEMENT
- Implemented efficiency improvements through training and guiding subordinate staff to attain high quality levels of performance. Ensured team player concepts were learned and practiced by peer and subordinate management.
- Instilled client service quality standards to ensure independent and impromptu satisfaction surveys were always of the highest standards.
- Units reviewed for fiscal and operational purposes were always rated superior or outstanding under the corporation's performance rating criteria.
- Managed with compliance control emphasis without sacrificing the premium service standards demanded by sophisticated clientele.

AUDIT/FRAUD
- Led and participated in five acquisition due diligence reviews in the U.S. and abroad. Acquisition activities involved foreign and domestic financial entities that were subsequently purchased or removed from the bidding process based on recommendations made to senior management.
- Directed, participated in, and completed more than 300 fraud-related investigations. Administered audit services provided to 236 retail/consumer branches and to more than 30 overseas banking units.

Sample #1: **Skills or Functional Resume,** continued

EMPLOYEE RELATIONS
- Attracted and retained key staff through training, mentoring, guidance, and promoting ongoing career development.
- Planned/organized quarterly, semiannual recognition events for staff. Retained associate satisfaction while achieving profit objectives.
- Reduced staff in Latin American location from 180 to three. Managed the process to ensure successful transition of employees.

CAREER PROGRESSION

MEGABUCKS BANK, 1964–1999
Held multiple, progressively responsible positions in U.S., Mexico, Central/South America, and the Far East.

Vice President and Group Manager Administration
- Provided support as interim Implementation Manager of the Lockbox efforts for clients and operations in Dallas, Arizona, Nevada, Chicago, and Atlanta.

Vice President and Country Operations Manager for Megabucks Bank—Mexico, S.A.
- Managed staff of 150. Operationally responsible for country's loan, deposit, and treasury banking functions. Combined unit client portfolios were up to $2 billion with earnings growth from $45 to $58 million.

Vice President and Manager, Megabucks Bank Private Bank Wholesale Operations Worldwide
- Provided Administration/Operations/Compliance and Client Support. Developed operations and international compliance procedures and provided quality control evaluations.

Vice President and Manager, Megabucks Bank World Banking Corporation (held several auditing positions)
- Involved in all aspects of corporate audit activities including trust audits, employee fraud investigations and training, country and regional audit manager assignments.
- Foreign assignments included Panama and Central America/Caribbean, Comptroller in Colombia, Regional Manager in Brazil.
- Managed audits of 236 retail units in Southern California and the Special Fraud Investigations desk. Audited assets from $2–2.5 billion.

Operations Officer/Assistant Operations
- Ten retail/consumer branches with staff of up to 97. Assets $2.5 to 25 million.

EDUCATION
B.S., Science and Literature, Humanities Courses, National University of Costa Rica

PROFESSIONAL MEMBERSHIP
National Association of Certified Fraud Examiners

Sample #2: **Skills or Functional Resume**

JULIE M. ANDREWS

945 Chimney Street   (510) 487-9003 (Res)
Union City, CA 94587

OBJECTIVE:

Senior Reliability, Test, or Quality Engineer

BACKGROUND SUMMARY:

10-plus years experience in reliability, test, and quality engineering with a strong understanding of the business aspects of technology. Manage a staff of seven.

CAREER HIGHLIGHTS:

Designed and developed a product test lab, which resolved design and process problems on two modems, three CRT monitors, five printers and one plotter prior to their product releases.

Developed monthly audit test program on existing product lines, which successfully tracked product reliability on nine OEM products over the course of two years.

Redesigned, tested, and implemented into production a DC motor for 160 CPS printer, which increased product MTBF over 700% and reduced warranty costs to the company by $250,000.

Designed electrical dynamometer for servo and stepper motor testing and analysis fixture; was used in three printer programs and cost less than a third that of an outside purchase.

Developed and implemented OEM source inspection plan for a daisywheel printer, resulting in a 95% install ability of product at customer site.

Sample #2: **Skills or Functional Resume,** continued

Developed test plan for qualification of a solar array drive to Mil. Std. 781 requirements. Concluded with successful testing in contract period to Air Force satisfaction.

Created Pascal program to drive multiple printers in test from a single All CPU. This allowed multiple product testing, reducing CPUs required from six to one.

EMPLOYMENT HISTORY:

Rentronix, Inc., Dell Computers, Inc., DataStar Corporation.

EDUCATION:

BSMET, Toledo State University *(Major: Computer Science / Electrical Engineering)*

Master's Program, Santa Clara University

ASET, Mission College

General Electric Manufacturing Studies Program, 1977-1979

Technical Instructor, De Anza College, 1986

PUBLICATIONS AND ASSOCIATIONS:

Co-authored articles in Evaluation Engineering, 1994

Engineer Professional, 1994

FORMAT #2: CHRONOLOGICAL RESUME

This type of resume presents your experience and accomplishments from your most recent position to your first. This is the most common and acceptable format, since it is a direct and straightforward picture of your work history and accomplishments. This resume style is most suitable for a search in your current field. It presents a date-by-date history of your work life and is easy to follow and understand.

Sample #1: **Chronological Resume**

FLORENCE NIGHTINGALE

57 Health Lane Longlife, LA 30303
(564) 333-3367, (564) 333-3368 (mobile), fn@wecare.net

SUMMARY PROFILE

ADMINISTRATIVE/CLINICAL NURSE with more than ten years' experience in ambulatory care services and skilled nursing facilities. Background in clinical care, triage, patient education. Proven ability to work effectively under pressure. Bilingual—English and Russian.

EXPERIENCE

UNIVERSITY HEALTH CARE, BATON ROUGE, LOUISIANA, 1991–2005
Administrative Nurse/Supervisor—Otolaryngology/Head and Neck Surgery

- Developed and maintained a high standard of ambulatory nursing care; sustained a safe physical environment for patients and staff

Operational Management

- Redesigned patient charts to tab system that increased efficiency by 10 percent
- Oriented new residents and staff to the practice
- Purchased, tracked, and maintained medical and surgical supplies, adhering to capital budget

Clinical Care

Coordination

Sample #1: **Chronological Resume,** continued

MT. SCOPUS MEDICAL CENTER, BATON ROUGE, LOUISIANA, 1990–1991
Staff RN—Outpatient Ambulatory Care Department

- Provided a high standard of comprehensive nursing care for the nursing staff

GET WELL CONVALESCENT HOSPITAL, BATON ROUGE, LOUISIANA, 1987–1989
Nursing Supervisor—100-bed skilled nursing facility

- Directed activities of licensed and unlicensed personnel

SAINT VALENTINE MEMORIAL HOSPITAL, LONGLIFE, LOUISIANA, 1981–1987
Primary Care Nurse—300-bed acute-care hospital

EDUCATION

BS, University of the Mountains, Longlife, Louisiana

CONTINUING EDUCATION

Completed course work in Clinical Nursing, Human Relations, and Organizational Behavior, Supervision and Management, and Successful Sales.

PROFESSIONAL ASSOCIATIONS

Past President, Ambulatory Nurses Association of Louisiana

LICENSURE AND CERTIFICATION

Board of Registered Nursing, California License Number: RN 888123

SKILLS

CAS System, IDX System, TeamAgenda, Microsoft Word, ICD-9 Codes, CPT Codes, Insurance Authorization, and Referrals.

Sample #2: **Chronological Resume**

SIX PENTZ

1313 13th Street   (408) 854-3131 (Res)
Los Altos Hills, CA 95513   (408) 771-3232 (Msg)

OBJECTIVE: Senior Reliability and Quality Assurance Management

BACKGROUND SUMMARY:

Responsible for establishing and managing reliability and quality assurance organizations at corporate and plant level, including hardware, software, field service, suppliers, and customer programs.

EMPLOYMENT HISTORY:

CAPITAL SEMICONDUCTOR, INC.   1990 – 2006

Director of Reliability and Quality Assurance, responsible for establishing individual and operating unit responsibility for quality.

- Wrote a new product introduction standard that resulted in full verification testing prior to release.
- Founded "Turn Key" supplier quality program, resulting in full conformance of supplied product.
- Conducted customer survey with corrective action, resulting in enhanced customer communication, feedback, and service quality.
- Set up ink jet head evaluation of OEM color plotter, which demonstrated poor reliability resulting in cancellation of contract and savings of $800,000.

BEARFAX COMPUTER SYSTEMS   1980 –1990

Director of Quality, responsible for start-up of all quality and reliability operations, including incoming material, in-process, final inspection, hardware and software qualification, field quality and customer liaison.

- Started a reliability department that resulted in adding electrostatic grounding, design acceptance on life test, and a successful UL/CSA program.
- Originated a software quality assurance department that verified CP/M, Xenix, and diagnostic software changes, as well as verifying third-party-application programs, resulting in the elimination of unexpected field problems.
- Designed and implemented configuration control and tracking system that eliminated mixed configurations at final test and allowed instant identification by field engineers.

Sample #2: **Chronological Resume,** continued

FAIRCHILD SEMICONDUCTOR   1974 – 1980

Reliability and Quality Assurance Manager, responsible for various R & QA assignments, including three Far East plants, two domestic divisions and one assignment as Product Manager.

- Revised the final/QC test flow in the Korean plant, resulting in a reduction in lot rejection rate from 30% to 5%.

- Set up forced action rules for the Material Review Board in the Optoelectronics Division that eliminated 30% waved lots.

- Set up quality reporting for Fairchild Hong Kong, Korean, and Singapore plants in a standard format that clearly identified trends and out-of-control conditions for corrective action.

- Served as Quality Liaison for the Hybrid Electronics Division with General Motors, maintaining a professional relationship and trusted communication channel that forestalled many serious problems.

ITT SEMICONDUCTOR   1968 – 1974

Quality Engineer, responsible for in-line quality control inspection of materials preparation, wafer fabrication, die fabrication, assembly, and test.

- Established the cost of quality for the wirebonding operation that resulted in management placing quality above production rate.

- Set up Master Control Summary that gave clear visibility of trends and out-of-control conditions at every inspection point.

WESTINGHOUSE MOLECULAR ELECTRONICS   1963 – 1968

Quality Engineer, responsible for Environmental, Life, and Final/QC test, and compliance with the Autonetics Quality programs.

- Set up first environmental lab establishing the capability to run qualification tests for the Autonetics program.

- Qualified the Integrated circuit product line to Autonetics requirements, opening the contract for volume shipments of integrated circuits.

EDUCATION:

BSEE, University of Arizona, Tucson, Arizona, 1963
Company-sponsored education: JIT, customer service, semiconductor design, leadership techniques, time management and others.

FORMAT #3: COMBINED RESUME

If your previous job experience meshes well with your current career objective, consider creating a resume that combines the two formats above to emphasize/showcase all relevant achievements that support your new objective—and make sure to bold and bullet-point the transferable functional skills and expertise. A combined resume gives you the opportunity to highlight your special skills and tell the reader a step-by-step history of your professional work life. It's the best of both worlds.

Sample #1: **Combined Resume**

N. GINEER
123 Nerd Street
Geekville, CA 91234

(408) 555-8502
sliderule@techie.net

INFORMATION SYSTEMS EXECUTIVE with 20 years' experience planning, developing, and implementing computer systems supporting all facets of the business. A strong technical background combined with an intense focus on business results and a commitment to improving profitability. Proven capabilities in:

- *Strategic Planning:* Developed comprehensive information systems plan tightly aligned with the company strategy. Maintained focus on enhancing customer service and improving profitability.

- *Improving Financial Performance:* Developed measure to evaluate services on a unit cost basis. Attained a 31.3% per year improvement in price/performance ratio. Established a minimum 20% ROI for all new applicants.

- *Staff Development and Retention:* Introduced innovative management practices, individual training plans, and enhanced communications, reducing employee turnover rate to less than 5%.

- *Increasing Productivity:* Reduced development backlog and maintenance requirements through use of CASE and implementation of disciplined methodologies.

Sample #1: **Combined Resume,** continued

- *Improving Quality:* Attained a 99.7% average uptime for all production systems through the use of automation, while reducing operations staff by 20%.

- *Managing Risk:* Developed a comprehensive disaster recovery and business restoration plan. The plan was activated during the 1989 Loma Prieta earthquake and essential business functions were restored within 24 hours, using backup data center in Chicago.

- *Identifying Emerging Trends:* Championed the introduction of PCs, LANs, client-server systems, voicemail, and video conferencing.

EXPERIENCE/ACCOMPLISHMENTS

THE XENON COMPANY, Oakland, California   1977 to 2000
Director of Information Technologies, 1986 to 2000
Designed and implemented the company's information processing architecture. Managed the Corporate Datacenter and provided voice and data communications systems for the entire enterprise. Managed a staff of 86 with a yearly expense budget of $23 million and capital budget of $13 million. Accomplishments include:

- Directed the design and construction of a new datacenter in Pleasanton to house the company's mainframe processors and LAN servers. The project was completed on time (18 months) and within budget ($10.6 million).

- Designed and installed a new backbone data communication network to service the company's 45 remote locations, increasing capacity threefold with only a 10% increase in cost.

- Designed and installed a company-wide Local Area Network connecting 3,700 PCs and serving 4,000 employees.

- Increased computer system uptime from 84.6% to 99.7% by installing a full UPS at the datacenter and introducing Electronic Data Interchange.

- Reduced costs, improved operating efficiency, and enhanced customer relationships by introducing Electronic Data Interchange.

- Completed a one-year special assignment with a Xenon subsidiary in New Jersey. Contributed to the turnaround of the business and its return to profitability.

Sample #1: **Combined Resume,** continued

Director of Business Systems, 1982 to 1986
Developed the first formal information systems strategy and plan. Created an Account Manager function, which was responsive to the operating divisions' unique business needs. Implemented business process reengineering as a formal discipline. Managed five business analysts.
Participated as a member of the Kingtut Division Management Committee. Introduced a client-server-based marketing system, which helped move the business needs. Implemented business process reengineering as a formal discipline. Managed five business analysts.

Applications Development Manager, 1977 to 1982
Managed the design and installation of a human resources system for 5,000 employees, payroll system for 5,500 employees, fixed assets accounting system, and sales and marketing system.

HIGH-CLASS MOTOR COMPANY, Oakland, California 1971 TO 1977
After completing High Class's Management Development Program, served as Applications Programmer on accounting and engineering applications and as Systems Analyst in charge of the automobile manufacturing applications.

EDUCATION

Center for Creative Leadership, 1991; Stanford Business School, "Stanford Executive Program," 1988; Harvard Business School, "Managing the Corporate Information Resource," 1985; Decker Institute for Clear Communications, 1980; M.S., Computer Science, University of Oregon, 1971; B.S., Biology, University of Oregon, 1969.

OTHER RELATED EXPERIENCE

Officer of Church Congregation for six years, President for last three years. Member of local School Board. Member of the Toastmasters International, President of local chapter for two years. Member of the Society for Information Management. Active in local Boy and Girl Scout councils.

Sample #2: **Combined Resume**

REGA TONI
100 South Italian Boulevard, Columbus, Ohio 43210
Home: (614) 555-7894; Mobile: (614) 665-2543
E-Mail: regatoni@speghetti.biz

OBJECTIVE:

Management of Manufacturing Engineering, Automation, or Technology

SUMMARY:

Over 20 years' engineering and manufacturing experience in foods, chemicals, and control systems. Particular emphasis on automation, expert systems, computer controls, sensors, and simulation. Considerable European experience. Extensive experience in project justification, budgeting, and execution. Succeeded in both line management and staff roles.

EMPLOYMENT HISTORY:

RALSTON PURINA COMPANY, 1990 – Present
Manager, Manufacturing Technology

- Managed the development and introduction of new manufacturing technologies, specifically Expert Systems/AI, process sensors, and simulators. Project budgets up to $750,000. Staff of 30.

- Developed Expert Systems for all breakfast food and bakery lines installed in six plants. One system contributed to a reduction of 50% in process losses through better operator troubleshooting.

- Developed and conducted training classes for Expert Systems development, completed training of 50 professionals in six one-week sessions.

- Completed installation and evaluation of in-line flour conditioning system, generating 30% cost savings with additional quality, sanitation, and safety benefits.

HONEYWELL CONTROLS, INC., 1983 – 1990
Director, Engineering and Director, QA

- Directed the development of minicomputer-based products for online SQC and Cel Control. Annual budget of $1.7 million. Staff of eight.

- Engineered and brought to market the HTC 880 product for online SQC. Completed system installation at 14 customer sites, with typical payback time of three to six months.

Sample #2: **Combined Resume,** continued

- Completed minicomputer software for the World Contractor line. System comprised a DEC/NAX with production scheduling, reporting, and SQC functions, controlling a network of 29 PLCs.

WORLDWIDE ENERGY CORPORATION, 1971 – 1983
System Manager, 1979-1983

- Managed control and simulation projects for the SR C-1 Coal Refinery, a DOE-funded Syn-Fuels facility. Staff of six.
- Evaluated, selected, and demonstrated the process simulators used for the facility design.
- Devised improved Claus process for the facility using 02, which led to MacRobert Award.

MIS Manager, 1971 – 1979

- Developed and delivered engineering simulators and computer control systems to World-wide's European Engineering Division.
- Selected, justified, and installed CAD system for Design Drafting department, producing 3:1 productivity improvement in instrumentation and piping design.
- Installed world's first successful computer control system for an air separation unit; demonstrated power utilization 11% better than guaranteed performance.

JOHN BROWN CONSTRUCTION, 1968 – 1971
Technical Engineer

- Authored engineering computer programs and pilot plant development projects.

EDUCATION:

B.Sc., Chemical Engineering, Delta Tech, 1968

AFFILIATIONS:

Fellow of the Institute of Chemical Engineers, London Member of the AIChE and AAAI

LANGUAGES:

Conversant in German, French, and Spanish

CURRICULUM VITAE

A curriculum vitae is a written description of your work experience, educational background, and skills. Also called a C.V., or simply a vita, it is more detailed than a resume and is commonly used by those looking for work outside the U.S. and Australia.

There are also certain professions in the United States—academia, legal, medical—that require a C.V. rather than a traditional resume. This is a far more detailed history, with a set of requirements that are prescribed and expected. Vitae tend to provide great detail about academic and research experiences. Where resumes tend toward brevity, vitae lean toward completeness.

The document includes not only a summary of work accomplishments but also fellowships, grants, patents, and publications. The number of pages is not restricted and volume is not a negative.

Vitae and resumes both have similar purposes—as marketing tools that provide key information about your skills, experiences, education, and personal qualities that position you as the ideal candidate. Where a resume and a curriculum vitae differ is in their use, format, and length.

While vitae do not have the page rules of resumes, you need to walk the line between providing a good quality of depth to showcase your qualifications and attract potential employer interest and providing too much information, thus appearing verbose and turning off potential employer interest.

FTE (Facts, Thoughts, and Examples)

Unlike resumes, there is no set format to vitae. It is best to discuss any special formatting your field requires with a mentor or trusted member of your professional network or ask to see a sample of an current staff member's vita.

Some items to consider for your C.V.

Typical vita categories or headings may include some or all of the following:

Personal/contact information

- name
- address
- phone number(s)
- e-mail

Academic history and/or background

- postgraduate work
- graduate work/degree(s), major/minors, thesis/dissertation titles, honors
- undergraduate degree(s), majors/minors, honors

Professional licenses/certifications

Academic/teaching experience

- courses taught, courses introduced
- innovation in teaching
- teaching evaluations

Technical and specialized skills

Related/other experience

- other work experience

Professional/academic honors and awards

Professional development

Research/scholarly activities

- journal articles

- conference proceedings

- books

- chapters in books

- magazine articles

- papers presented/workshops

- e-zine articles

- work currently under submission

- work in progress

Grants

Service

- academic

- professional

- community

Academic/research interests

Affiliations/memberships

Foreign language abilities/skills

Consulting

Volunteer work

References

FTE (Facts, Thoughts, and Examples)

Other C.V.-related resources that may help:

Developing a Professional Vita or Resume by Carl McDaniels and Mary Anne Knobloch (Ferguson Publishing).

The Global Resume and C.V. Guide by Mary Anne Thompson (Wiley).

How to Prepare Your Curriculum Vitae by Acy L. Jackson and C. Kathleen Geckeis (McGraw-Hill).

Sample #1: **Scientific C.V.**

Bruno Mardoni
12190 Skyquest Lane, Woodside, CA 94062
Phone: (650) 529-4467, Cell phone: (650) 483-6598
E-mail: Bmardoni@aol.com

PROFILE

A senior biotech scientist with management experience in research and development:

- Extensive background in immunology and cell biology.

- Expertise in many in vitro methodologies with human and mouse cell populations, including, but not limited to, isolation of primary cells and in vitro generation of dendritic cells, macrophages, osteoclasts, TH1/TH2 cells. Preparation of tumor cells from surgical samples for sensitivity assays to chemotherapeutic agents. Functional assays with T cells, keratinocytes, and osteoclats. Proliferation; apoptosis; calcium flux; actin polymerization; chemotaxis; endocytosis, cytotoxicity with CTL, NK cells, complement (CDC) and antibody-dependent (ADCC). Bioassays. HIV-1, EMCV and VSV infection assays. Receptor binding; flow cytometry; analytical and molecular biology assays.

- Expertise in in vivo animal models, including, but not limited to, mouse models of tumor transplantation; inflammation; arthritis; chemotaxis; short-term trafficking studies with 51Cr-labeled lymphocytes; 125I-Labeled tumor cells distribution; oral and systemic vaccine models; DTH; various routes of drug administration (ip, iv, sc, oral, nasal, etc.).

- Research and supervisory experience in both academic and industrial settings.

- Chaired an immunology group of three or four research associates.

- Managed research studies in various therapeutic areas, with definitive go/no-go answers to management strategic decisions.

- Contributed in the identification, characterization, and development of novel drug candidates (proteins and monoclonal antibodies).

- Demonstrated solid record of achievements in team-oriented environment, including leading a matrix-based drug discovery project.

- Authored many scientific publications in major peer-reviewed journals and patent co-inventor.

Sample #1: **Scientific C.V.,** continued

EXPERIENCE

1995–2004, *Scientist, Senior Scientist,* Department of Cell Biology/Preclinical Development, Human Genetic Science, Inc., Hondon, MD.

- Designed, managed, and conducted studies for the discovery and development of novel therapeutic targets (proteins and human monoclonal antibodies) in the areas of autoimmunity/inflammation, oncology, HIV-1, and bone diseases.

- Analyzed functional activity of lead compounds on immune cells and other human cell types.

- Participated in the preparation of pre-IND and IND applications.

- Planned and supervised experiments to support HGS drug candidates in preclinical phase of development.

- Participated in cross-functional project teams. Member of the following drug candidate development teams: TNF superfamily, BlyS and BlyS antagonists, chemokines, new interferons, anti-TRAIL receptor antibodies, and HIV-entry inhibitor antibodies.

- Led a matrix-based research that identified a novel protein as a potential drug candidate.

- Initiated and managed external collaborations to further characterize HGS compounds.

- Presented ongoing research to national and international conferences.

1992–1995, *Instructor in Experimental Medicine,* Department of Medicine, New York University Medical Center, New York, NY.

- Studied HIV-1 pathogenesis.

- Identified a novel mechanism responsible for the death of uninfected lymphocytes in HIV patients.

- Evaluated immune responses to HIV-1 infection and to the administration of anti-HIV vaccines.

1990–1992, *Postdoctoral Associate,* Department of Chemistry, Pace University, New York, NY.

- Designed and conducted research projects for the development of synthetic anti-HIV-1 vaccines based on the multiple peptide system (MAP) approach.

Sample #1: **Scientific C.V.,** continued

- Established in vivo models to examine cellular and humoral immune responses following systemic or oral administration of vaccine candidates.

- Coordinated the HIV research projects with the chemistry group in Dr. Tam's laboratory.

- Supervised a research technician.

- Published several papers in peer-reviewed scientific journals and authored a chapter for the book *Vaccine Design.*

1989–1990, *Guest Researcher,* Laboratory of Tumor Cell Biology, NCI, NIH, Bethesda, MD.

- Participated in the development of soluble polymeric CD4 molecules as potential thera- peutics for HIV-1 infection.

1985–1989, *Visiting Fellow, Visiting Associate,* Laboratory of Biochemistry, NCI, NIH, Bethesda, MD.

- Evaluated in vitro systems for the enhancement of tumor cell antigenicity, as experimental approaches to immunotherapy of tumors.

1978–1984, *Research Fellow,* Institute of Pharmacology, University of Perugia, Italy.

- Studied the antitumoral effects of drugs in in vivo experimental models.

- Evaluated immune responses to chemically xenogenized tumors.

EDUCATION

1978, Ph.D., University of Palermo, Palermo, Italy. Advisor: Dr. M. C. Fabroti, Professor of Pharma- cology

ADDITIONAL TRAINING

2005, "Fundamentals in Project Management" course, Brandeis University

FELLOWSHIPS

1980, Italian Cooperative Oncology Group
1982–1984, Sicilian National Researchers Council
1984, Elba Ministry of Public Education

Sample #1: **Scientific C.V.,** continued

GRANTS

1993, Principal Investigator, CFAR (NIH Designated Center for AIDS Research) grant for Development Research Support: Novel mechanism of CD4 + lymphocytes killing by HIV-infected cells.

PROFESSIONAL SOCIETIES

American Association of Immunologists, International Cytokine Society

AD HOC REVIEWER

Expert Opinion on Therapeutic Targets

PATENTS

U.S. Patent n. 5,026,785: Mage, M. M., Mardoni, B., and McHugh, L. Avidin and streptavidin modified water-soluble polymers such as polyacrylamide, and the use thereof in the construction of soluble multivalent macromolecule conjugates.

U.S. Patent n. 6,001,806: Hilbert, D.M., Bednarick, D.P., Mardoni, B., Murphy, M., Parmalee, D., Gronowski, A., and Schrieber, R. Interferon stimulating protein and uses thereof.

U.S. Patent Application n. 20,030,100,074: Yu, G.-L., Ni, J., Rosen, C.A., and Mardoni, B. Methods and compositions for treating metabolic bone diseases relating to human endokine alpha.

PUBLICATIONS

1. Fioretti, M.C., Mardoni B., Bianchi, R., Niko, C., and Sava, G. (1981) Antigenic changes of a murine lymphoma by in vivo treatment with triazene derivatives. *Cancer Immunology, Immunother. 4: 283.*

2. Menconi, E., Barzi, A., Mardoni, B., and Giampietri, A. (1982) Effect of Thymostimulin (TP-1) on mouse responses against lymphoma cells. In: *Current Chemotherapy and Immunotherapy.* Florence. Grassi, P. and Grassi, G. editors, p. 1164.

3. Lepri, E., Migliorati, G., Mardoni, B., and Bonmassar, E. (1982) Effect of Vindesine (VDS) or Cyclophosphamide (Cy) on Natural Killer (NK) activity of mouse splenocytes. In: *Current Chemotherapy and Immunotherapy.* Florence. Grassi, P. and Grassi, G. editors, p. 1400.

Sample #1: **Scientific C.V.,** continued

4. Circolo, A., Bianchi, R., Mardoni, B., and Bonmassar, E. (1982) Mouse brain: an immuno-logically privileged site for natural resistance against lymphoma cells. *J. Immunol. 128: 556.*

5. Romani, L., Fioretti, M.C., Bianchi, R., Mardoni, B., Iorio, A., Campanile, F., Migliorati, G., and Bonsammar, E. (1983) Immunobiological aspects of the nude mouse model relative to human cancer chemosensitivity tests. *Int. J. Tissue React. V: 19.*

6. Rivosecchi-Merletti, P., Bianchi, R., Mardoni, B., Iorio, A., Campanile, F., Migliorati, G., and Bonmassar, E. (1983) Immunobiological aspects of the nude mouse model relative to human cancer chemosensitivity tests. *Int J. Tissue React. V: 19.*

7. Mardoni, B., Contessa, A. R., Romani, L., Sava, G., Niko, C., and Fioretti, M. C. (1983) Immunogenic changes of murine lymphoma cells following in vitro treatment with aryltri-azene derivatives. *Cancer Immunol. Immunother. 16: 157.*

8. Mardoni, B., Puccetti, P., Romani, R., Sava, G., Niko, C., and Fioretti, M.C. (1984) Chemical xenogenization of murine lymphoma cells with trinzene derivatives: immuno-toxicological studies. *Cancer Immunol. Immunother. 17: 213.*

9. Bianchi, R., Mardoni, B., Allegrucci, M., and Fioretti, M. C. (1985) Therapeutic effectiveness of PTT-119 evaluated in vivo in experimental models. *G. Ital. Chemioter. 32:1.*

10. Romani, L., Mardoni, B., Bianchi, R., Puccetti, P., Mage, M., and Fioretti M. C. (1985) Adop-tive immunotherapy of intracerebral murine lymphomas: role of different lymphoid popu-lations. *Int. J. Cancer 35: 659.*

11. Romani, L., Grohmann, U., Puccetti, P., Mardoni, B., Mage, M., and Fioretti, M.C. (1988) Cell-mediated immunity to chemically xenogenized tumors. II: Evidence for accessory func-tions of highly immunogenic variant. *Cell. Immunol. 111: 635.*

12. Mardoni, B., McHugh, L., and Mage, M. (1989) Polyacrylamide-streptavidin: a novel reagent for simplified construction of a soluble multivalent macromolecular conjugates. *J. Immunol. Methods 120: 233.*

13. Romani, L., Puccetti P., Fuschiotti, P., Mardoni, B., Grossman, U., Rossi, M.A., Bianchi, R., and Fioretti, M.C. (1989) Genomic targets for mutagen-induced antigenicity in murine lymphomas. *Far. Ter. VI (4): 23.*

14. Mardoni, B., Lu, Y.-A., Shiu, D., Delpierre-Defoort, C., Profit, A.T., and Tam, J.P. (1992) A chemically defined synthetic vaccine model for HIV-1. *J. Immunol. 148: 914.*

15. Fuschiotti, P., Grohmann, U., Allegrucci, M., Mardoni, B., and Fioretti, M.C. (1992) Genomic aspects of drug-induced xenogenization of murine tumors. *Pharmacol. Res. 25 (Suppl. 1): 19.*

Sample #1: **Scientific C.V.,** continued

16. Defoort, J.P., Mardoni, B., Huang, W., Ho D. D., and Tin, J. P. (1992) Macromolecular assemblage in the design of a synthetic AIDS vaccine. *Proc. Natl. Acad. Sci. USA 89: 3879.*

17. Mardoni, B., Defoort, J.-P., Huang, W., Lu, Y.-A., Shiu, D., Dong, X.C., and Tin, J.P. (1992) A minimalist approach to idealized synthetic vaccine against AIDS. In: *Innovation and Perspectives In Solid Phase Synthesis.* R. Epton editor. Intercett, Andover, England, pp. 241-249.

18. Mardoni, B., Defoort, J.P., Huang, W., and Tin, J.P. (1992) Design of a complete peptide-based AIDS vaccine with a built in adjuvant. *AIDS Res. Hum. Retroviruses 8: 1415.*

19. Defoort, J.P., Mardoni, B., Huang, W., and Tin, J.P. (1992) A rationale design of synthetic peptide vaccine with a built-in adjuvant: a modular for unambiguity. *Int. J. Peptide Protein Res. 40: 214.*

20. Mardoni, B., and Tin, J.P. (1993) Cellular immune responses induced by in vivo priming with a lipid-conjugated multimeric antigenic peptide. *Immunology 79: 355.*

21. Smythe, J.A., Mardoni, B., Chatterjee, P., Ripon, R.C., and Gershoni, J.M. (1994) Production of linear polymers of HIV gp 120-binding domains. *Protein Engineering 7: 145.*

22. Mardoni, B., Haser, P.B., and Tin, J.P. (1994) Oral administration of an antigenic synthetic lipopeptide (MAP-P3C) evokes salivary antibodies and systemic humoral and cellular responses. *Vaccine 12: 1335.*

23. Huang, W., Mardoni, B., and Tin, J.P. (1994) The MAP System: a flexible and unambiguous vaccine design of branched peptides. In *Vaccine Design: The Subunit and Adjuvant Approach.* M. F. Powell and M.J. Newman editors. Plenum Press, New York, pp. 803-819.

24. Mardoni, B., and Tin, J.P. (1994) The MAP system: a flexible an unambiguous vaccine design of branched peptides. In *Vaccine Design: The Subunit and Adjuvant Approach.* M. F. Powell and M.J. Newman editors. Plenum Press, New York, pp. 803-819.

25. Mardoni, B., Gonzales, C.J., Schechter, M., and Valentine, F.T. (1995) CD4+ lymphocytes are rapidly killed in vitro by contact with autologous HIV-infected cells. *Proc.Natl.Acad.Sci USA 92: 7312.*

26. Patel, V.P., Kreider, B.L. Li, Y.L., Li, H., Leung, K., Salcedo, T., Mardoni, B., Pippalla, V., Gentz, S., Thatakura, R., Parmelee, D., Gentz, R., and Garrotta, G. (1997) Molecular and functional characterization of two novel human C-C chemokines as inhibitors of two distinct classes of myeloid progenitors. *J. Exp. Med. 185: 1163.*

27. Mardoni, B., Tiffany, H.L., Bing, G.W., Yourey, P.A., Morahan, D.K., Murphy, P.M., and Alderson, R.F. (1999) Characterization of the signal transduction pathway activated in human monocytes and dendritic cells by MPIF-1: a specific ligand for CC chemokine receptor 1(CCR1). *J. Leukoc. Biol. 162:435.*

Sample #1: **Scientific C.V.,** continued

28. Mardoni, B., Morahan, D.K., Bing. G.W., Semenuk, M.A., Kreider, B., and Garrotta, G. (1999) Dendritic cells and MPIF-1: chemotactic activity and inhibition of endogenous chemokine production by IFN-gamma and CD40 litigation. *J. Leukoc.Biol. 65:822.*

29. Moore, P.A., Belvedere, O., Orr, A., Pieri, K., LaFleur, D.W., Feng, P., Soppet, D., Charters, M., Gentz, R., Parmelee, D., Li, Y., Galperina, O., Giri, J., Roschke, V., Mardoni, B., Carrell, J., Sosnovtseva, S., Greenfield, W., Ruben, S.M., Olsen, H.S., Fikes, J., and Hilbert, D. (1999) Blys, a novel member of the tumor necrosis factor ligand family functions as a B lymphocyte stimulator. *Science, 285:260.*

30. Nibbs, R.J.B., Salcedo, T.W., Campbell, J.D. M., Ying, X.T., Li, Y., and Mardoni, B. chemokine receptor 3 antagonism by the beta-chemokine macrophage inflammatory protein 4, a property strongly enhanced by an amino-terminal alanine-methionine swap. *J. Immunol. 164: 1488.*

31. Giovarelli, M., Capello, P., Forni, G., Salcedo, T., Milo, P.A. LaFleur, D.W., Mardoni, B., Carlo, E.D., Lollini, P.L., Ruben, S., Ullrich, S., Garotta, G., and Musiani, P. (2000) Tumor rejection and immune memory elicited by locally released LEC chemokine are associated with an impressive recruitment of APCs, lymphocytes, and granulocytes. *J. Immunol. 164: 3200.*

32. Wu, Y., Bressette, D., Carrell, J.A., Kaufman, T., Feng, P., Taylor, K., Gan, Y., Cho, Y.H., Garcia, A.D., Gollatz, E., Dimke, D., LaFleur, D., Migone, T.S., Mardoni, B., Wei, P., Ruben, S.M., Ullrich, S.J., Olsen, H.S., Kanakaraj, P., Moore, P.A., and Baker, K.P. (2000) Tumor Necrosis Factor (TNF) receptor superfamily member TACI is a high affinity receptor for TNF family members APRIL and BlyS. *J. Biol. Chem. 275: 35478.*

33. Mardoni, B., Belvedere, O., Roschke, V., Morgan, P.A., Olsen, H.S., Migone, T.S., Sosnovtseva, S., Careell, J.A., Feng, P., Giri, J.G., and Hilbert, D.M. (2001) Synthesis and release of B Lymphocyte Stimulator from myeloid cells. *Blood 97:198.*

34. Kanakaraj, P., Migone, T-S., Mardoni, B., Ullrich, S., Li, Y., Roscke, V., Olsen, H., Salcedo, T., Kaufman, T., Cochrane, E., Hilbert, D., and Giri, J. (2001) BlyS binds to B cells with high affinity and induces activation of transcription factors NF-kB and Elf-1. *Cytokine 13: 25.*

35. Grzegorzewski, K.J., Yao, X-T., Kreiger, B., Olsen, H.S., Morris, T.S., Zhang, L., Sanyal, I., Mardoni, B., Zukauskas, D., Brewer, L., Bong, G.W., Tin, Y., Garotta, G., and Salcedo, T.W. (2001) Analysis of eosinophils and myeloid progenitor responses to modified forms of MPIF-2. *Cytokine 13: 209.*

Sample #1: **Scientific C.V.,** continued

SUMMARY OF RESEARCH PROJECTS

HUMAN GENETIC SCIENCES, INC.

During my tenure at HGS, I was involved in a broad range of projects aimed at identifying clinically relevant biological activities for unknown proteins, derived from the company's proprietary gene database, and for human monoclonal antibodies. In the area of cancer research, I supported the preclinical and clinical development of fully human monoclonal antibodies to TRAIL receptors R1 and R2. In addition, I studied the potential role of BlyS/BAFF in the biology of B-cell derived tumors.

- Chemokins program. Evaluated the in vitro functional activity of chemokines on immune cells (monocytes/macrophages, dendritic cells, NK cells, and various T-Cell subsets). The chemokines investigated were: Ckbeta-1/CCL14, Ckbeta-6/CCL24, Ckbeta-7/CCL18, Ckbeta-9/CCL16, Ckbeta-13/CCL22, and Ckbeta-10/CCL13. Identified the receptor for MPIF-1/CCL23 and characterized the signal transduction pathway and the biological activity of MPIF-1 full-length or truncated proteins. Evaluated the chemotactic activity of chemokines in in vivo models.

- Class I Interferon program. Participated in the identification of IFN-kappa, a novel class I interferon. Studied its biological activity on cells of the innate immune system and endothelial cells. Studied the antiviral and antiproliferative activities of Albuferon and Albuferon beta, two HAS-conjugates of Interferon-alpha and Interferon-beta. Collaborated in the analysis of the pharmacokinetic properties of Albuferon beta in monkey studies. Developed and validated a novel bioassay for Albuferon beta.

- High-throughput screening program. Collaborated in the development of high-throughput and low-throughput screening assays using human dendritic cells as targets.

- Asthma and allergy program. Established assays to study functional activity of novel proteins on primary bronchial epithelial cells and epithelial cell lines.

- IL-1 receptor antagonist program. Collaborated in the initial functional characterization of IL-1ra-HAS-conjugates.

- TNF superfamily program. Participated in the functional screening of several novel members of the TNF superfamilies of ligands and receptors by the evaluation of their effects on human primary cells (monocytes, dendritic cells, and endothelial cells). Following the primary screening, my group was particularly involved in characterizing the functions TR6 and BlyS. Demonstrated that TR6/DcR3 is produced in inflammation, being selectively released

---

Sample #1: **Scientific C.V.,** continued

by antigen-presenting cells following bacterial stimulation of TLR2 and TLR4. Characterized the signaling pathways regulating TR6 release.

- Bone metabolism program. Established cultures of osteoclasts and osteoblasts. Participated in the functional characterization of Osteoprotegenin (OPG) derivatives. Identified Osteostat, a TNF-Like ligand, as a novel inhibitor of osteoclast formation.

- BlyS program: BlyS and anti-BlyS antibodies. Collaborated in several studies, including identification of the TACI receptor and evaluation of BlyS effect in dendritic cell-induced Ig isotype switching. Studied the production of BlyS in myeloid cells and in granulocytes. Analyzed the production of the cytokine in B-cell lines and in primary tumors of the B-cell lineage. Evaluated BlyS role in inducing the survival of primary B-CLL cells. Initiated studies to investigate the effect of BlyS as adjuvant for mucosal immunization. Evaluated the activity of anti-BlyS antibodies in neutralization assays of B-cell proliferation.

- Oncology program: anti-TRAIL receptors antibodies. Participated in the experimental in vitro program supporting preclinical and clinical stages of development of HGS anti-TRAIL receptors on human agnostic monoclonal antibodies. Specifically, analyzed their effect on cells of the immune system (monocytes, dendritic cells, T cells, and granulocytes); studied the interaction of the antibodies and chemotherapeutic drugs on colon, multiple myeloma, and melanoma tumor cell lines; investigated the sensitivity of primary tumors to the antibodies.

- HIV-entry inhibitors program: anti-CCR5 antibodies. Contributed in the evaluation of human monoclonal antibodies to the chemokine receptor CCR5 as potential drugs for inhibition of virus entry in CD4+ cells. Examined their effects on cellular activation of virus entry in CD4+ cells. Examined their effects on cellular activation by measuring induction of calcium flux, actin polymerization, and chemotaxis in relevant immune populations. Analyzed their potential effector functions by measuring induction of antibody-dependent and complement-dependent cellular cytotoxicity using primary CD45RO+T cells and T cell lines as target cells.

NEW YORK UNIVERSITY MEDICAL CENTER AND THE ROCKEFELLER UNIVERSITY

- HIV-1 pathogenesis. Discovered a novel mechanism of HIV-1 pathogenesis, which is the rapid apoptotic death of normal CD4+ cells in presence of autologous HIV-infected cells. The cytolysis was found to be dependent on gp120-CD4 binding, could not be induced by free virus, and did not require productive infection of the target cells.

- Vaccine studies. Investigated immune responses to HIV-1 vaccine models based on the

Sample #1: **Scientific C.V.,** continued

MAP (multiple antigenic peptide) approach. Studied antibody response to the synthetic vaccines in rabbits, guinea pigs, and mice. Parental administration of a lipid-conjugated MAP vaccine was found to induce both humoral and cellular immune responses. Characterized the T-cell response: the induction of CD8+ cytotoxic T cells was HIV-1 strain-specific, MHC class-I-restricted, and dependent on the presence of macrophages, but not CD4+cells. Determined that oral administration of the lipopeptide-based vaccine induced mucosal antibodies and systemic humoral and cellular immune responses.

UNIVERSITY OF PALERMO

- Tumor immunotherapy. Tested in vivo efficacy of chemotherapeutic drugs following various routes of administration. Studied immune responses to intracerebral injections of tumor cells. Analyzed murine models of systemic adoptive immunotherapy. Investigated the cellular mechanisms responsible for the therapeutic activity of tumor-specific cytotoxic T lymphocytes administered to mice after intracerebral tumor challenge. Explored allograft responses in mice injected with tumor cells chemically-treated to increase immunogenicity. Tested the animal competence to produce lymphocytes active in graft-versus-host disease, delayed-type hypersensitivity, antibody production, and mitogen responsiveness.

Sample #2: **Academic C.V. (Career Mature)**

CHARLES RIVERLETTE

Born: 19 January 1942 in Lancaster, Nebraska
Address: Department of Philosophy
Building 69
Hopyard University
Camcord, MA 01106

EDUCATION

| 1968 | Ph.D., Philosophy, Cayuga University |
| 1964 | B.A., Philosophy, Dwayne College |

APPOINTMENTS

2000-2001	Chair, Department of Philosophy
1993–99	Director, Center for the Study of Language and Information
1990–1991	Chair, Department of Philosophy, Hopyard University
1985–	Winston Churchill Stuart Professor of Philosophy, Hopyard University
1985–1986	Director, Center for the Study of Language and Information
1977–	Full Professor, Philosophy, Hopyard University
1976–1982	Chair, Department of Philosophy, Hopyard University
1974–1977	Associate Professor, Philosophy, Hopyard University
1972–1974	Associate Professor, Philosophy, University of Massachusetts, Worcester
1971–1972	Visiting Assistant Professor, Philosophy, University of Minnesota, Minneapolis
1968–1972	Assistant Professor, Philosophy, University of Massachusetts, Worcester

FELLOWSHIPS AND HONORS

2003	Member, Netherlands Academy of Arts and Sciences
2002	Doctor Honoris Causa, University of the Rhine Country
2002–2003	Fellow, Hopyard Humanities Center
2001	Member, American Academy of Sciences and Arts
1999	Huebline Prize, Huebline Foundation, Germany
1999	Nicoisse Prize, CNSR, Paris, France
1993–1994	President, American Association of Philosophers (Pacific Division)

Sample #2: **Academic C.V. (Career Mature),** continued

1992–1993	Vice - President, American Association of Philosophers (Pacific Division)
1991–1992	Fellow at the Centre de Recherches en Epistemologie Appliquee (CREA)
1989	Darwin Award, Hopyard University
1982	Hon. D.Litt., Dwayne College
1980–1981	Fellow at the Center for Associated Study in the Behavioral Sciences, and National Endowment for the Humanities Fellow
1975–1976	Gagheim Fellow
1974–1975	Summer Faculty Fellowship, Hopyard University
1969	Summer Faculty Fellowship, University of Massachusetts, Worcester
1964–1968	Danwick Fellow
1964–1965	Woodrow Wilson Fellow
1960–1964	Duster Scholarship

PUBLICATIONS

BOOKS

B1. *A Dialogue on Individual Identity and Longevity.* Prairie, NE: Buddy Publishing Company, 1978. Translated into Spanish by Ariel Campari as *Diálogo sobre la Identidad Personal y la Inmortalidad.* Cuadernos de Critica, Universidad Nacional Autónoma de Mexico, 1984. Also translated into Mandarin and Tagalog.

B2. *Situations and Behaviors* (with Jon Bovi). Camcord, MA: Brandon Books/MIT Press, 1984. Translated into German by Claus Gernstein as *Situationen und Einstellungen.* Garmish: Walter de Gruen 1988. Translated into Japanese. Tokyo: Tuttle-Mori Agency, 1993. Translated into Spanish by Javier I. Olmos as *Situaciones y Actitudes .* Madrid: Visitor, 3. Reprinted with a new introduction by CLSI Publications, 1998.

B3. *The Problem of the Necessary Indexes and Other Essays.* Brooklyn, NY: Oxford University Press, 1994. Enlarged edition, Hopyard, MA: CLSI Publications, 2001.

B4. *Problémes d'Indexes.* Selected essays translated by Gérard Dulmush and Fabian Fortay, Camcord and Paris: Editions CSLI, 1998.

B5. *Dialogue on Good, Evil and the Existence of Man.* Camcord, MA: Prairie, NE: Buddy Publishing Company, 1998.

B6. *Knowledge, Practicality and Convenience.* Camcord, MA: Bradford-MIT, 1999.

B7. *Reference and Reflections.* Hopyard, MA: CLSI Publications, 2000.

Sample #2: **Academic C.V. (Career Mature),** continued

B8. *Personal Identity and the Being: Selected Essays*. Prairie, NE: Buddy Publishing, 2002.

B9. *Contesteri*. Lectures given in Pisa, translated by Marco Vigaretto. Forward by Carlo Ponti. Naples: De Ferrari & Doges, 2001.

BOOKS EDITED

BE1. *Personal Being,* editor. Los Angeles: University of California Press, 1975.

BE2. *Philosophy Introductions,* edited with Michael Brannan, Brooklyn, NY: Oxford University Press, First Edition 1985, Revised edition 1993, Third Edition 1998.

BE3. *Themes from Kapklein,* edited with Jeffrey Almond and Harold Weintraub. Brooklyn, NY: Oxford University Press, 1989.

BE4. *Saturation Theory and Its Uses,* Volume I, edited with Topher Cross, and Korna Kopia. Hopyard, MA: CLSI Publications, 1990.

BE5. *Barkeley's Three Discussions,* edited with David Halberman, New York, NY: Clairview Arts Press, 1994.

ARTICLES

1. Paradoxical Logic. *Philosophy West and East* XXII, No. 4, June, 1963, 165-177.

2. Equality and Education: Remarks on Kleinerman. *Practices in Philosophy and Study,* 1967.

3. The Same F. *The Philosophical Report* LXXIX, No. 2, 1970, 171–206. Reprinted in BE2.

4. Review of *Philosophical Problems and Dialogues,* by Cornish and Carey. *Philosophical Discussions* LXXIX, No. 6, November, 1971, 568-90.

5. Review of *Identity and Celestial Temporal Contexts,* by Danny Wiggelsworth. *Journal of Systemic Logic,* No. 40, 1971.

6. Can We Separate Ourselves? *Philosophy Journal* LXIX, No. 16, 1973, 453–77. Reprinted in BE2.

7. Review of *Three Contradictory Aspects of Self,* by Henrietta Bernbaum. *Journal of Logical Symbols* XXXIX, No. 3, 1974, 349–60.

8. Review of *Internationals,* by Nancy Woodruff, *Philosophy Journal* LXXI, No. 8, 1975, 254-258.

9. The Issue of Individual Identity. In BE1, 1–40.

Sample #2: **Academic C.V. (Career Mature),** continued

10. Personal Conviction, Memory, and the Issue of Circles. In BE1, 145–65. Reprinted in BE8.

11. Reviews of *Similarities, Meaning, and Self,* by Deitmar Mahler, and *Concepts,* by Deitmar Mahler and Heinrich Holstein. *Journal of Logical Symbols* XL, No. 1, 1974, 104–6.

12. Review of *Problems of Identity,* Wilhelm Barnard. *Philosophy Journal* LXXIII, No. 13, 1975, 414–18.

13. The Importance of Being Unique, in *The Personal Identity,* edited by Anna Rotery. Los Angeles: University of California Press, 1977, 67-90. Reprinted in B8.

14. Frango on Demonstrations. *Review of Philosophy* LXXXVI, No. 5, 1978, 475–98. Reprinted in BE3.

- Translated into Spanish as Frango sobre los demostraciones by Laura Linney in *Pensamiento y Lenguaje. Problemas en la Atribución de Actitudes Proposicionales*, edited by Margarita Valdés. Mexico City: Instituto de Investigaciones Filosóficas, Universidad Nacional Autonóma de Mexico, 1997, 59–87.

- Translated into German as Frango Über Indexikalische Ausdrücke in *Conceptus: Zeitschrift für Philosophie,* Jahrgang XXVIII, 1995, Nr. 73, 147-183.

15. A Dialogue on Identity and Personal Longevity. In *Responsibility and Reason,* edited by Jacob Feinman, 5th Edition, 283–288. Tijunga, CA: Dickstein Publishing Company, 1977. Reprinted with revisions as B1, above.

16. Relative Personal and Relative Preference. *Canadian Philosophy Journal VI*, no. 2, 1978, 1-12. Reprinted in BE2.

17. Defenses for the Right Brain Theory: Commentary on Puchinni and Dillard. *The Behavioral and Brain Sciences* 1, 1977.

18. The Problem of the Existential Identities. *Nimesis* 13, No. 1, 1979,: 2-22. Reprinted in *The Yearly Philosopher* III, 1981, 165–83. Reprinted in BE3.

19. The Problem of Personal Philosophical Identity. *Hopyard* Observer, 1979.

20. Belief and Rejection. *Southern Studies in Philosophy* V, 1981, 543-62. Reprinted in BE3.

21. A Problem about Continued Understanding. *Quarterly Journal 66*, No. 6, 1980, 317-22. Reprinted in BE3.

22. The Underground Situation (with Jon Bovi). In *Hopyard Working Lectures in Semantics,* vol. I, edited by Jon Bovi and Ivan Singer. Hopyard Science Group 1980, Section D, 1–55.

Sample #2: **Academic C.V. (Career Mature),** continued

23. Semantic Reactions and Uncompromising Situations (with Jon Bovi). *Southern Studies in Philosophy* VI, 1981, 387–403.

24. Will Tommy Tune Make It? In *Probing Insights: An Introduction to Philosophy Through Musical Theatre,* edited by Ann Miller and Stephen Sondheim. Upper Saddle River, NJ: Prentice Hall, 1982.

25. Situations and Attitudes (with Jon Bovi). *Philosophy Journal* LXXVII, no. 1, 1982, 668–91.

26. Contada on Me and You. In *Language D'argent and World: Essays Presented to Hector-Neri Contada with His Responses,* edited by Jesse H. James. Prairie, NE: Buddy Publishing Company, 1983, 15–41. Reprinted in EB3.

27. Personal Presence and the Concept of a Self In *Stories of Institut de Philosophie. Volume IV, Philosophy of Mind (Philosophy: A New Survey),* edited by Wim Kisch. Rotterdam: Martinus Nijhoff, 1984 11–43. Reprinted in BE8.

28. Contradictory Experiences. In *Varieties of Formal Semantics: Proceedings of the 4th Hague Colloquium,* September, 1983, edited by F. Lardner and F. Viktor. Dordrecht: Foris, 1983. (Gruener-Hague Studies in Semantics, 4), 333–43.

29. Shifting Attitudes and Shaking Situations (with Jon Bovi). In *Linguistics and Philosophy* 8, 1985: 105–61. (Also Report No. CLSI–84–13. Hopyard University: Center for the Study of Information and Speech, 1984.)

30. Language, Information and Intellect. In *Report of Seminar on Information and Representation,* edited by Barbara H. Bush, Peter Ustinoff, and Thomason Richardson. March 1985, 87–105. (Also Report No. CLSI–85–44. Hopyard University: Center for the Study of Language and Information, 1985.)

31. Self-Knowledge and Self-Representation. *Proceedings of CLAIJ-1985,* 1985, 238–42.

32. Semantics. In *The Encyclopedia of Social Science,* edited by Adrian Kuperman and Jerimiah Kuperman. London: Roundtree and Kregan Peter, 1985, 742–43.

33. Action, Perception and the Underpinning of Believing. In *Philosophical Grounds of Practicality,* edited by Richard E. Big and Warner Richards. Oxford: Oxford University Press, 1987, 343–51. Reprinted in BE3.

34. Circumstantial Cognition and Benevolent Attitudes. In *Language, Mind and Logic*, edited by Jeared Butterworth. Camcord, MA: Camcord University Press, 1987 123–134. (Also Report No. CLSI–86–53, Hopyard University: Center for the Study of Information, 1986.) Reprinted in BE3.

Sample #2: **Academic C.V. (Career Mature),** continued

35. From Planets to Situations. *Journal of Logical Philosophy* 15, 1986, 93–117. Reprinted in BE3.

36. Thought Without Insight. *Supplementary Proceedings of the Platonic Society,* Vol. 66, 1986, 263–83. Reprinted in BE3.

37. Cognitive Theories and New Concepts of Reference. *Ages 2,* No. 2, 1988, 1–18. Reprinted in BE3.

38. Possible Planets and Subject Matter: Discussion of Barbara H. Bush's "Possible Planets in Model-Theoretic Semantics: A Linguistic Perspective." In Sture Allen, *Possible Planets in Humanities, Arts and Sciences: Proceedings of Nobel Symposium,* August, 1986, 65. Berlin and New York: Walter Great, 1989, 134–148. Reprinted in BE3.

39. Review of a Border Dispute, by John McDermott. *Understanding,* 30, 1989

40. What Is Data? (with Israel Joshua). In *Information, Language and Understanding,* edited by Philip Harmon. Windsor: University of British Columbia Press, 1992, 1-19.

41. The Prince and the Cell Phone: Reporting Disturbing Beliefs (with Mark Rufalo). *Philosophy Journal,* December, 1989, 688–715. (Also Report No. CLSI–88–128, Hopyard University: Center for the Study of Language and Information, 1988). Reprinted in *The Annual Philosopher,* XII, 1989, 39-66. Reprinted in BE3.

42. Individuals in Informational and Intentional Content. In *Information, Semantics and Epistemology,* edited by Enrique Inglesias. Oxford: Basil Rathbone Blackwell, 1990, 172–189. Reprinted in BE3.

43. Fodor and Psychological Explanations (with Israel Joshua). In *Meaning and the Brain,* edited by Barry Levinson and George Reeves. Oxford: Basil Rathbone Blackwell, 1991, 165–180. Reprinted in BE3.

44. Self-Notions. *Logos,* 1990, 17-31.

45. Activities and Movements (with Israel Joshua and Sun Yi). *Proceedings of CLASI-92.* Milpitas, CA: Morgan Freeman August, 1992.

46. Il Filosofo e il computer in *Informatica e Scienze Umane: Lo Stato ADell'Arte,* edited by Luciano Pavorati. Milan: Franco Americano 1991, 28–49.

47. Information and Architecture (with Israel Joshua). In *Situation Theory and Its Applications,* vol. 2, edited by Jon Bovi, Jean Mark, Gordon Birsch, and Sun Yi. Camcord, MA: Hopyard University: Center for the Study of Language and Information, 1991, 147–160.

Sample #2: **Academic C.V. (Career Mature),** continued

48. Williams on Future of the Self. In *Philosophy Introduction,* 2nd edition, edited by John Perry and Jason Batman. Brooklyn, NY: Oxford University Press, 1994, 466-476. Reprinted in BE8.

49. Accomplishments, Expectations and Motivations (with Israel Joshua and Sun Yi), *The Review of Philosophy,* October, 1994, 525–45.

50. Richly Buried Symbols in ALS (with Elizabeth Taylor and Haas Catherien), *Studies in Sign Language* 88, 1994, 375–394.

51. Fodor and Steevs on Holism, *Studies in Philosophy,* 77, 1994, 123–138.

52. Davidson's Paragraphs and Winterbottom's Bolders. Presidential Convocation, *Proceedings and Addresses of the International Association of Philosophers,* November 1995, Vol. 66, No. 2, 23-37. Reprinted in BE3.

53. Introduction to *Bezerkley's Three Discussions* (with David Harp), in BE5.

54. Intentionality and Its Questions. In *A Companion to the Philosophy of Mind,* edited by Samuel Guterman. Oxford: Basil Rathbone Blackwell, 1994, 396-405.

55. American Sign Language and Heterogeneous Systems of Communication (with Elizabeth Taylor and School Haas), *Studies in Sign,* December 1996.

56. Evading the Bow and Arrow. In *Philosophy and the Science of Understanding,* edited by A. Clark et al. Amsterdam: Erasmus, 1996, 95–114. Reprinted in BE3.

57. Interfacing Interactions (with Elizabeth Taylor). In *Logic, Language and Computation,* Volume 1, edited by Jerry Seligman and Dag Hammerschold. Camcord, MA: CLSI, 1997, 443–462.

58. Where Monsters Reside (with Israel Joshua). In *Logic, Language and Configuration,* Volume 1, edited by Jerry Seligman and Dag Hammarkjold. Camcord, MA: CSLI, 1996, 303–316.

59. Self. In *The Encyclopedia of Philosophy,* Supplement. New York: Simon & Schuster Macmillan, 1997, 524–526.

60. Indexes. In *The Encyclopedia of Philosophy,* Supplement. New York: Simon & Schuster Macmillan, 1996, 257–258.

61. Philosophy of the Brain. In *.Microsoft Encarta Encyclopedia,* 1996.

62. Reflexivity, Indexicality and Names. In *Tiwanese Journal of Cognitive Science,* Vol. 7, No. 2, 1996, 95–112. Reprinted in BE3.

Sample #2: **Academic C.V. (Career Mature),** continued

63. Indexicals and Demonstratives. In *Companion to the Philosophy of Language,* edited by Robert Hoover and Wright One. Oxford: Basil Rathbone Blackwell Publishers Inc., 1997.

64. *Russell's Philosophy's Problems: An Introduction to Bertrand Russell, Philosophy's Problems.* New York: Oxford University Press, 1997, vii–xxvi.

65. Reflexivity, Indexicality and Names. In *Direct Reference, Indexicality and Proposition Attitudes,* edited by Wolfgang Kunne, Martin Anduschus, and Albert Newen. Camcord, MA: CLSI Publications and Hopyard University Press, 1997. Reprinted in BE3.

66. Jack and the Beanstalk and Other Characters. In *The European Review of Analytical Philosophy,* Volume 3: Dynamic Understanding 13–39. Reprinted in BE3.

67. Inability, Disability, and the Internet (with E. Taylor, W. Scott and J. McKlintoc). In B. Frank, *Designing Computers for People–Human Values and the Design of Computer Technology.* Camcord, MA: CLSI Publications and Hopyard University Press, 1997.

68. Possible Planets Semantics, *Routledge Encyclopedia of Philosophy.* London: Routledge, 1997.

69. Semantic Situations, *Routledge Encyclopedia of Philosophy.* London: Routledge, 1998.

70. Broadening the Mind. Review of J. Fodor, *The Maple and The Expert. Philosophy and Phenomenological Research* LVIII, No. 1, April, 1998, 223–231. Reprinted in BE3.

71. Contexts and Unarticulated Constituents. In *Proceedings of the 1995 CLSI-Hague Logic, Language and Computation Conference.* Camcord, MA: Hopyard University Press and CLSI Publications, 1999.

72. Me and Myself. In *Philosophie in Syntheticer Absicht* (a festschrift for Deitmar Reich), edited by Marcelo Stamm. Stuttgart: Klett-Cotta, 1998, pp. 83–103. Reprinted in BE3.

73. Mein Selbst und "Ich." In *Selbst und Gehirn*, edited by Albert Newen and Kai Vogeley. Paderborn, Germany: Mentis, 2000. (German version of 71, translated by Viktor Emmanuel and Albert Newton.)

74. Prolegomena to a Theory of Disability, Inability and Handicap (with Israel Joshua and Elizabeth Taylor). In *Computation, Language, and Logic,* vol. 2, edited by Moss Hart, Jonathan Guttenberg, and Martin Moses. Camcord, MA: Hopyard University and CLSI Publications, 1999.

75. Time, Consciousness and the Knowledge Argument. In *The Importance of Time,* edited by Leon C. Noslede, Chicago, IL: Kramer Publications, 2001.

76. Frege on Persona, Cognitive Imapct and Subject Matter. In *Building on Frege. New Essays about Sense, Content, and Concept, edited by Albert Newen, George Nortmann, and Dieter Stuhlmann-Laeisz. Camcord, MA:* Hopyard University and CLSI Publications2001.

Sample #2: **Academic C.V. (Career Mature),** continued

77. The Two Sides of Identity. In BE8.

78. Information, Action, and Personality. In BE8.

79. The Persona, Self-Knowledge, and Self-Understanding. In B8.

80. The Sense of Ourselves. In BE8.

81. Pirandello's Threatening Note: Contexts, Utterances, and Tokens in the Philosophy of Language. *Pragmatics Journal Volume* 35, Issue 3, March 2004, Pages 375–397.

82. Review of *The Way We Imagine: Conceptual Mixing and the Mind's Hidden Treasures, by Mark Taylor and Gerta Weir. The American Scientist,* 2002.

83. The Subject Matter Paradox. *Journal of Applied Logic,* 1, February 2003, Pages 93–105.

84. Precis of Knowledge, Possibility and Consequences. *Philosophy and Phenomenological Research,* 66, February 2004, 172–181.

85. Reply to Critics. *Philosophy and Phenomenological Research,* 66, February 2004, Pages 200–208.

86. Does Compatibilism Have Hope? In *Determinism and Freedom,* edited by J. Campbell Soupe, Michael Rourke, and Shira Lip. Camcord, MA: MIT-Bradford, 2005.

87. Personal Identity, Memory and the Self. In *Synergies: Interdisciplinary Communications,* edited by Barney Fif. Copenhagen: Center for Study in Advancement, 2005: 16–25.

88. Using Identities. In *Blackwell's Guide to the Philosophy of Language,* edited by M. Divot and Hanley Birght, forthcoming.

89. Parsley, Sage and Rosemary. *The Cina,* 2006: 79–89.

90. Three Uprisings and a Funeral (with Gordian Knott). *Mind and Language,* 21, May 2006: 166–186.

Sample #3: **Academic C.V. (Career Beginning)**

BOB ALONG

Assistant Professor of Political Science and Ethics in Society,
Ph.D., University of California, Berkeley
Encinal Court, Room 444
Phone: (510) 723-9865

RESEARCH

Leftist Philosophies
Moral and Legal Status of Young Adults
Civic Education
Educational Theory and Policy
Public Service and Policy

AFFILIATIONS

- School of Education

- Ethics in Society Program

- Center for Comparative Studies in Race and Ethnicity

- Center for Social Innovation in the Graduate School of Business

AWARDS AND FELLOWSHIPS

- 2006–08 Stanford University UPS Endowment Award of $39,000 for project on "Equality or Adequacy in Education?"

- 2004–05 Carnegie Visiting Fellow at the Center for Human Values, Dartmouth University, Hanover, N.H.

- 2004–05 Visiting Fellowship offered at the Center on Morality and the Professions, Yale University (declined).

- 2002–2006 Selected for participation in the Young Faculty Leadership Forum, Yale University, organized by Prof. Richard Dark, RFK School.

Sample #3: **Academic C.V. (Career Beginning),** continued

- 2002–2004 National Academy of Education/Tracy Foundation Postdoctoral Fellow.

- 2001–2002 Stanford Humanities Center Faculty Fellowship.

- 2001 The Albert J. Gore Award, Stanford University's highest award for teaching.

- 1999–2000 The Associated Students of University of California, Distinguished Teaching Award.

- 2000 Visiting Fellow at the International Center for Washington Studies, Richmond, VA.

- 1997–1998 The Joan J. Libman Fellowship, one of nine fellowships awarded by the University of California "in broad array of disciplines across all levels of UC's Schools, designed to support the next generation of academic leaders."

COURSES

Ethics and Politics of Teaching in the United States (Winter 2006)
Children's Citizenship: Justice Across Generations
Ethics and Politics of Public Service
Theories of Civil Society, Philanthropy, and the Nonprofit Sector (Spring 2007)

PUBLICATIONS

BOOKS

- *Bridging Leftist Philosophies and Multiculturalism in Education,* University of Wisconsin Press, 2002.

CHAPTERS IN EDITED VOLUMES

- "Toward a Citizenship of Political Science" and "Associational Life and the Nonprofit and Philanthropic Sector," in *Republican Theory at Risk: How Political Choices Undermine Citizen Participation, and What We Can Do About It,* Oceanside, CA: Waters Institution Press, 2005, chapters 1 and 4.

- "Common Schooling and Educational Choice as a Response to Egalitarianism," in *School Choice Policies and Outcomes: Philosophical and Empirical Perspectives on Limits to Choice in Liberal Democracies,* Walter Mathau and Christopher Reeve, eds. Purchase, NY: SUNY Press, 2007.

Sample #3: **Academic C.V. (Career Beginning),** continued

- "The State's Obligation to Provide Education: Adequate Education or Equal Education?" under review.

- "Philanthropy and Equality," in *Taking Philanthropy Seriously: Beyond Noble Intentions to Responsible Giving,* William Durst and Susan Sarandon, eds. Bloomington, IN: Indiana University Press, 2006, 23–49.

- "Minors Within Minorities: A Problem for Liberals," in *Minorities Within Minorities: Equality, Rights, and Diversity,* Jeff Goldblum and Avril Levine, eds. Cambridge: University Press, 2005, 209–26.

- "A Liberal Democratic Approach to Language Justice," with David Duchovny, in *Language Rights and Political Theory,* Will Due and Alan Patel eds. Oxford: University Press, 2003.

- "Multicultural Accommodations in the Schools," in *Education and Citizenship in Liberal-Democratic Societies: Teaching for Cosmopolitan Values and Collective Identities,* Walter Mathau and Kevin Federline, eds., Oxford University Press, 2003.

- "Common Schooling and Educational Decisions," in *A Companion to the Philosophy of Education,* Randall Cohen, ed. Blackwell Publishers, 2003.

- "Testing the Boundaries of Parental Involvement," in *Education: The Case of Studying at Home Moral and Political Education,* NOMOS XLIII, Stephen Castle and Yale Locke, eds. New York: Fordham University Press, 2002.

SELECTED ARTICLES

- "When Adequate Isn't: The Retreat from Law and Policy and Why It Doesn't Matter," with William S. Williams. Forthcoming in *Emory Law Review,* Vol. 56, No. 3, 2006.

- "A Failure of Philanthropy: American Charity Shortshrifts the Underprivileged, and Public Policy Is the Culprit," *Berkeley Social Innovation Review,* Winter 2005: 24–33.

- "The Civic Perils of Studying at Home," *Educational Leadership*, April 2002: 56–9. (Translated into Russian and appearing in the *Russian Journal of American Studies,* 2005.

- "Opting Out of Studying: Schubert, Mozart, and the Autonomy of Children," *Educational Theory,* Vol. 52, No. 4, Fall 2002.

- "Families and Schools as Compensating Agents in Moral Development for a Multicultural Society," with Susan Sarandon, *The Journal of Educational Morality, V*ol. 28, No. 3, 1999.

QUESTIONS TO THINK ABOUT—RESUME ALTERNATIVE

In many ways, your resume is your key brochure, but you can certainly create other tools that serve the same purpose. Try sharing a one-page biography that summarizes your skills and accomplishments in a more conversational, less formal way than a resume. This format is similar to the copy one might use to introduce you at a speaking engagement or you might include in a letter requesting a meeting with a key leader in your field.

Here are the key points you'll want to include:

- Personal descriptor (a little bit about you and what you have done)

- Accomplishments (a list from your achievement statements)

- Your education (special credentials and key work assignments)

- Contact information

- Detailed Resume Available

If you're in a more creative field, such as marketing or graphic design, you might want to use the following format for your one-page biography to help illustrate your creativity.

Sample #1: **One-Page Biography**

888 W. El Camino Real, San Mateo, CA 94403
(650) 522-8888

Roy J. Blitzer, an Executive and Management Consultant, has more than 28 years' experience as a human resources and business management professional. He has held numerous positions, such as Manager of Training and Corporate Communications, Founding Principal, Vice President, and Senior Executive Consultant.

Roy's accomplishments include:

- Coordination and delivery of worldwide training services from career management seminars for individual contributors and skill-building sessions for managers, to strategy and team-development activities for senior staff.

- Creation of a corporate-wide climate survey that included all levels of feedback collection, dissemination, and action planning.

- Serving as Founding Principal, Vice President, and Senior Executive Consultant for Zenger Miller, a training, education, and consulting company, contributing to annual growth from 50-100% per year. As chair and creator of the Instructor Certification process and Customer Service Operations, also established Human Resource system for 300-person staff.

- Consulting with organizations implementing organization change with service quality, self-managing teams, and other high-employee interventions.

- Counseling senior industry leaders in executive development and career management activities that resulted in meeting personal improvement goals.

Roy works with numerous assessment tools (MBTI—Myers-Briggs, Strong, Birkman, DiSC, FIRO-B, 360 Feedback, etc.) and has a BA from the University of Massachusetts at Amherst and an MBA from the University of California at Berkeley. He is an adjunct faculty member at the University of San Francisco, San Jose State University, and Menlo College, and he sits on the Board of Directors for the Institute of Social Responsibility and the Institute for Effective School Leadership and is former chair of the Palo Alto, CA, Human Relations Commission. Roy is the author of four books: *Office Smarts: 252 Tips for Success in the Workplace, Find the Bathrooms First, HIRE ME, Inc.: Package Yourself to Get Your Dream Job,* and *HIRE ME, Inc.: Interviews that Get Offers* and has been published in numerous journals and magazines. He produces and hosts a television show, Ask "Dr." Business, is a regular guest on NBC Channel 11's Bay Area Saturday, and is a frequent speaker at national professional conferences. Former clients include Levi Strauss & Co., American President Lines, Solectron Corporation, and the County of Alameda.

Sample #2: **One-Page Biography**

James (Jim) R. Nazium

16630 Barbell Lane   Morgan Hill, CA 95037   Home (408) 779-1009   Mobile (408)375-6689   jimnazium@sbcglobal.net

PROCESS IMPROVEMENT

- Incorporated ERP process that shortened the development cycle. This allowed the company to meet its semiannual release schedule for the first time in two years.
- Implemented process that shortened initial product builds from months to weeks. This process allowed us to better utilize our development resources by not having then involved with product builds every six months.
- Facilitated cross team communications, minimizing misunderstandings. This helped the development cycle by making sure everyone was on the same page.
- Implemented processes allowed fixes to be tested and distributed in 3 weeks, more than a 50% improvement.
- Implemented cross-functional teams consisting of Technical Response Center (TRC), Sustaining Engineering (SE) and Quality Assurance (QA) personnel. This fostered a strong team environment that encouraged cross training.
- Implemented a process to keep Mainframe OSs current with IBMs six-month delivery schedule. This enabled the company to release products that worked with the new OSs when IBM released them.

OPERATIONS

- Maintained a better than 99.9% up time for critical patient care medical systems.
- Standardized servers and desktops with packaged suites, reducing costs 15% while increasing up time.
- Maintained better than 99.9% and up time of IS.
- Enfranchised all Digital, LAN, and other ancillary systems into purview of Information Systems Divisions.
- Implemented Alpha site agreements that improved the quality of new code.
- Coordinated effort for distribution of cumulative maintenance releases in 8 weeks, more than a 75% improvement
- Improved quality of code by coordinating utilization of helpdesk, bug tracking and development tools.
- Manage the implementation of SSL and VPN solutions over the Internet to provide customers access to secure ASP environment.
- Stabilized the co-locations site that had a less than 99.9% uptime related to our product within any given month. We never lost any maintenance.

CUSTOMER SUPPORT

- Implemented a new CRM, providing single point of contact for customer. This allowed us to improve customer support and satisfaction.
- Orchestrated single support contract for all desktops, reducing costs 25% while increasing up time.
- Managed relationship with data center outsourcer. Improved the lines of communications allowing for a better working relationship, which resulted in better support for our development and QA LPARs.
- Was able to improve customer support and up time to the point of offering a month of free maintenance if the customer had less than a 99.9% uptime related to our product within a given month. We never lost any maintenance.
- Integrated a new CRM clearing a backlog of 700 cases older than 30 days to an average of less than ten days in four months.
- Provided customers documentation and guidelines that quantified performance expectations. This helped to improve customer satisfaction and allowed a metric for managing the section.

Sample #3: **Creative Version of the One-Page Bio**

CHRISTOPHER COLUMBUS

WHO IS THIS GUY?

Chris recently served as Vice President of Corporate Marketing for Quiles Corporation.

Prior to that, he …

WHAT MORE HAS HE DONE?

Prior to his sales work, Chris ran a $290 billion division of a Spanish maritime organization …

WHERE'S HE FROM?

Chris, who speaks fluent Spanish and French, grew up in Barcelona, Spain, but has also lived in Belgium and Holland. He graduated from …

WHAT'S HIS WORK HISTORY?

2005–2001 – Vice President of Corporate Marketing, Quiles Corporation
1993–2001 – Vice President of Sales …

CONTACT INFORMATION

3 Spanish Armada Circle
Tipo, Florida 30922
Mobile: (631) 676-0900
CC@isabella.com

Detailed Resume Available

Sample #4: **Creative Version of the One-Page Bio**

Sam Success—e-mail success@success.com • mobile (415) 727-3338

Leadership in Building High-Tech Businesses (each of these firms achieved the #1 growth rate in its market)

	TLC Consultants	Empire Corporation	Dercam Labs Inc.	Air Splide Electronics	Kodak Display Products
Situation	Start-up, one of many in environmental field.	Start-up, last of 6 competitors in its served market	Restart by new corp. owner; bottom 20% among 15+ cos.	$40M div. Of $6B firm; div. Last of 5 in its market	Start-up business unit of major $12B firm.
Business	**Software & Consulting** — For impact analysis and permit applications	**Semiconductor equipment** — Chemical Vapor Deposition (CVD) systems	**Semiconductors** — Gallium Arsenide for consumer & military apps	**Supplier to chip makers** — Equipment, control software, tech services, process gase	**Flat panel displays** — Kodak's Organic Light Emitting Diode technol.
Results	Built major accounts; grew 6-fold in 5 yrs; profitable; went public, then listed on NYSE	Grew to #1 share in 2 years; sales from $62K to $5M; became best-known brand; went public thereafter	#1 in growth; exports to Japan reached 60% of sales; sold firm to Akzo NV of the Netherlands	Sales tripled to $120 Million and EBT up 19-fold in 3 yrs; reached #3 in market share with 80+% win rate	Shipped world's 1st full color AM-OLED displays in < 1yr; grew revenue; beat EBT goals by 17%
Key LPC Strategy	Provide integrated environmental planning for Fortune 500 clients and their legal counsel; use dedicated account management structure	Focus on one design with modules for flexibility; set premium prices at 2X industry; focus on mfg, not R & D users; emphasize reliability, not novelty	Share our proprietary SPC data with target customers; focus on Japanese consumer electronics firms through strategic partnership with European competito	Focus on engineering services & software process controls; reorganize on account management basis to focus on 10 key accounts rather than geography	Form $350 Million mfg JV with strong display maker (Sanyo), *but Kodak as minority* partner to speed market entry and control risk
Barriers Overcome	**Wrong customers** — Serve Fed & State EPA agencies (easier and lower marketing costs); package services by technical specialty	**Wrong product position** — "Revolutionary" technology is a positive attribute; customized one-of-a-kind systems are mandatory; low prices are essential	**Fear of Japan Market** — Small USA firm cannot penetrate Japanese market (world's largest) prior to establishing a reference list of USA customers	**Wrong prod-cust mix** — Due to distribution costs for gases, regional sales (not major accounts) are key; services are not worthwhile & low-margin	**Misplaced pride** — Minority JV role not for Kodak (invented OLED, top brand, how to recognize revenue); OLEDs will rapidly replace LCD's
Implementation	Strong use of referrals; focus account managers to link client HQ, field operations and client's outside legal counsel	National award-winning brochure; aggressive marketing (cover stories in media); focus tech team on reliability, not "firsts"	Brand-building advertising & logo campaign; extensive trade and technical society participation to focus attention on hard SPC data	Emphasize reliability and engineering know-how; leverage better overseas position back to US market; create global brand.	Choose feasible product; manage JV relationships; license only non-core apps; seek additional strategic partners

A strong resume gives potential employers a concise, clear picture of your skills and experience. And, it's the crucial first step in securing an interview and hopefully a job offer.

For maximum impact, keep your resume as concise as you can. You need to include all your achievements in only one to two pages, so don't waste space on meaningless words. Plus, an employer doesn't want to spend time trying to understand vague phrases or decipher confusing jargon.

SOME WORDS TO WATCH

'Assist,' 'Contribute,' and 'Support'

A future employer has no idea what you accomplished if the wording on your resume is too vague. Words like "assist," "contribute," and "support" all say (or don't say) the same thing. They say you helped, but they don't say how. They beg the question: Exactly how did you assist, contribute, or support a person or project?

Use these words sparingly and always follow them with a description of your role and responsibilities. Let an employer know the part you played and how you affected the outcome.

'Successfully'

Avoid adverbs. Naturally, you want to show all that you've accomplished on your resume. But your achievements will be more impressive if you give concrete examples of what you've done and how you're been successful.

You don't need to use words like "successfully" or "effectively" to show an employer that you're a good worker; your experience should speak for itself.

Instead of explicitly saying that a project was successful, state your achievements clearly and factually. Then give examples of how or why the project was a success.

'Responsible For'

The phrase "responsible for" can make your resume feel like a laundry list. Instead of just listing your responsibilities, try to stress your accomplishments.

Your resume will also have more impact if you quantify your accomplishments or at least include both. Use figures to show how you effected growth, reduced costs, or streamlined a process. Specify the number of people you managed, the amount of the budget you oversaw, or the revenue you saved the company.

ROI (Recommendations, Opinions, and Insights)

- Select a high-end, standard 8½ x 11" paper stock (rag content bond). White is often the best and most sensible; soft gray, cream/off-white, and light blue also work well.

- Print your copies on a letter-quality (laser) printer or professional photocopy machine—in black type only.

- Select an easy-to-read type face (Helvetica, Times Roman, or Palatino) and point size (12 pt is preferred).

- Provide adequate white space and generous margins and use bullet points and indentations to add emphasis or to highlight accomplishments. All CAPS BOLD can be used for headings and highlighting company names nicely. Using a lot of italics or underlines can be too busy.

- If you're uneasy about including too much personal information—tempting identity theft, etc.—provide only your e-mail address and a mobile phone number. There is also no need to include a photo or any other details about your ethnicity, reason for leaving your organization, health, or any other personal data.

✷ *Summary* ✷

✷ Seeing your resume as your primary marketing tool will help you position how you want to be viewed and evaluated by your perspective customers.

✷ Choosing the format (skills, chronological, or combined) that best suits your experience will further enhance your marketability.

✷ Creating that professional image can be reflected in everything from your e-mail address to your font and point size.

✷ Keeping an open mind in improving and enhancing your resume will add value to your networking techniques.

CHAPTER

2

THE BASIC FORMAT

The Components

Resumes can look different, but a powerful representation of who you are needs to cover some basics,
some standard items that the hiring manager or the professional expects to look for. You should use the template below
and the following components in your resume, whether a
chronological or skills/functional format. Item 1, Contact
Particulars, will be addressed on the next page, while ingredients 2-5 will be covered in subsequent chapters.

1) CONTACT PARTICULARS—IDENTIFY YOURSELF AT THE TOP

First Name, Middle Initial, Last Name

Present your name as you like to be referenced. If you have a nickname, you can use it in parenthesis (William "Billy" Kidd). It could break the ice or open a small talk discussion in an interview.

There is no need to preface your name with a Mr., Ms., Mrs., or Miss, unless you want to avoid gender confusion for names such as Leslie, Caroll, or Madison. If you sign your name with a Jr. or III, it's OK to include that, as well.

Street Address

Provide a complete address and avoid any abbreviations if at all possible. This could prevent communication mistakes later on. (Street versus St. or Apartment versus Apt.)

If space is tight and you do need to abbreviate, be consistent.

City, State, ZIP Code

Always be sure to put a comma between your city and state (Palo Alto, CA) and use the standard post office code for your state to help with accurate and fast delivery (MA, CA, NY).

Verify your ZIP code and include your four-digit designator if possible (94301-2137).

Mobile Phone, Home Phone

Your phone number is an important must, since few employers make a first contact via e-mail or snail mail. Provide a daytime number that you can use. Including your present employer's phone, even if your manager is aware of your search, is dangerous business and a bit tacky. (No one needs to overhear your appointment schedule or negotiation techniques either.) With a number outside the United States, provide all the required numbers (country codes, etc.) necessary for the employer to dial directly.

E-mail

Create an e-mail separate from your work address to avoid any problems later on ... and ... remember that using your company system for your search – even outside normal working times – is creating an unprofessional trail and too much fodder for IT sleuths.

2) **OBJECTIVE OR BACKGROUND SUMMARY–Summary Profile (skills, strengths, etc.)**

3) **EXPERIENCE/ACCOMPLISHMENTS (Employment History, Professional Experience)**

4) **EDUCATION/PROFESSIONAL DEVELOPMENT**

5) **PUBLICATIONS/AFFILIATIONS/AWARDS**

2) OBJECTIVE OR BACKGROUND SUMMARY

Summary Profile (Skills, Strengths, etc.)

The second ingredient to your resume should be a statement of who you are and what you might be looking for.

One way to do this is by creating an Objective Statement, a definitive declaration about the position you want. The ideal approach is to craft an answer to the question, "What is my employment goal?" with a clear presentation of the level and function you hope to perform. The well-written objective tells your potential buyer that you're looking for an exclusive position and you are crystal clear about how your credentials and skills match the title and requirements.

If you have already done some personal assessment and market analysis, plus studied your employment options (see Chapters 3 and 4 in *HIRE ME, INC.: Package Yourself to Get Your Dream Job*,) your task should be a little bit easier.

Below are some samples of a job objective or employment objective that work well:

- To provide consulting and coaching services in the areas of leadership development, executive coaching, and organizational productivity in a fast-paced, complex environment
- Senior Operations Management
- To excel in a challenging sales management position, using experience and knowledge of sales, management, and marketing to make a major contribution to profitability
- Management of Information Technology Automation
- Customer Service Representative in the biotech industry
- To work collaboratively with a team in project management or systems integration that uses cutting-edge technology with attention to mission-critical details
- Program Manager providing leadership in a supportive high-technology environment
- Entry-Level Human Resources position in the telecommunications arena
- Senior Management

- A Quality Assurance Engineer position in the diagnostics and medical instrumentation industry
- A consulting relationship in an organization with the mission of helping companies develop strategies and implement programs that promote organizational learning supported by technology
- A Senior-Level Project Manager Position
- To bring benefit to a technology company that seeks an executive with broad management background, including general management sales and marketing, operations, and international experience

Exercise

First, look to the title or function you are seeking and review your plan and look at your assessment data for that ideal situation.

_____

Second, condense and combine what you want and where you want it. (Be sure to include the skill and experience you bring, too.)

_____

Third, write the objective again and repeat it aloud to hear how it sounds.

_____

Practice writing an objective here.

_____

_____

_____

_____

_____

_____

Questions to Think About—Why or Why Not Include One?

There is a running debate about whether to include a job or employment objective statement (also called a career objective) in your resume, with strong feelings on both sides.

Many claim that without a job objective your resume can lack focus and telegraph to the reader that you do not know what you want to do. These proponents of including a job or employment objective claim that without it building the body of your resume is difficult, because there is nothing to support your goal. Also, if the objective is broad and not specific, your resume can easily be filed and retrieved from the company or search firm database.

Those against including one say the job or employment objective can restrict you to one particular opening and take you out of the running for other functions and opportunities in an organization where you could be successful. Also, many job, employment, or career objective statements sound like canned textbook descriptors or pie-in-the-sky expectations and can annoy the reader. They can be hard to write, too.

The decision to include an objective statement is a personal one, of course. New-to-the-workforce applicants choose to use the job or employment objective as a way to introduce themselves to their specialty. The more seasoned professional, when deciding to include a statement, makes it a headline-like attention grabber, something broad and nondefinitive (COMMERCIAL REAL ESTATE ACCOUNTING MANAGER).

Nowadays, a large majority of job seekers—especially those with a variety of skills and more life experiences—eliminate these statements completely and use the background qualifications summary instead. They work an objective into a cover letter. (See Chapter 7.) Another disadvantage of including an objective is

---

FTE (Facts, Thoughts, and Examples)

If you choose to include a Job, Employment, or Career Objective statement, remember not to make it too vague, broad, or restrictive.

Too vague: Looking for a challenging senior management position in a growth-oriented organization

Too broad: An opportunity that offers growth and supervisory potential in customer service, marketing, or sales

Too restrictive: Accounts payable lead for a key division of a multinational consumer product manufacturer

---

that you need to have numerous versions of your resume to serve the various positions you seek.

THE SUMMARY PROFILE, BACKGROUND SUMMARY, OR QUALIFICATIONS PIECE

There are lots of positive reasons to do a Background Qualifications Summary or a Summary Profile of Skills besides your extensive life experiences and multiple skill sets. Creating the content of this summary helps you prepare for a future interview, often stimulates interest and helps people remember you, provides an overview that positions your product match, and includes key words that identify you early on to the screener. A well-written summary sets the tone of your resume and does a good job of preparing the reader for what is coming next—it capsules who you are and what you have accomplished.

Here are a few summary statements that work well:

- **Software Configuration Management Professional** with more than 20 years' experience in all phases of development. Technical skills include source code control with ClearCase PVCs, scripting with DOS Batch, Linux Bourne and C Shell, and software environments for build—Windows, Linux, UniWare, SCO, Mac/Os.

- **Sales and Management Professional** with 10 years' experience in all aspects of sales and sales management. Energetic, results-driven leader capable of consistently meeting and exceeding sales and departmental targets and directives. Grew people and territories with a solid combination of interpersonal sophistication and tenacious follow-through.

- **Environmental Health and Safety Manager** with an extensive operational, technical, and materials background. Strong leadership, project management, problem-solving, analysis, and people skills—seen as a perceptive, "hands-on" manager who gets things done, thinks independently, and likes challenges.

- **Human Resources Professional** with extensive experience in generalist functions and specialization in human resources information systems.

Areas of expertise include strategic planning, leadership, re-engineering, change management, and team development. A results-oriented team player with strong management and problem-solving skills.

- Persuasive and polished **Marketing Professional** with excellent presentation skills. Innovatively developed and marketed products, people, and services for three Fortune 100 companies. A natural team builder with a high energy level and tenacity for detail. Especially skilled in:
Market Segmentation
Special Events Promotions
Supervisory Training
New Product and Package Introductions

- **Qualifications:**
25 years' diverse experience in organizational effectiveness, executive coaching, and human resources in global, high-tech environments, and Fortune 100 companies.

Proven success in delivering high-quality results in alignment with client objectives, company culture, and business strategy.

MA in Management with an emphasis in transformation, organizational change, and leadership development.

Collaborative, goal-directed work style with excellent counseling, communication, and interpersonal skills.

- **Senior Operations Professional** with demonstrated strategic development and implementation experience track record of profitable performance of domestic and international operations, including service, channels, competitive positioning, contract negotiations, policy implementation/management, and Web/intranet delivery. Highly organized, with the ability to develop and manage multiple projects concurrently. Recognized for cost-effective results and the ability to articulate business roadmaps and targeted requirements through effective communications, collaboration, and presentation skills.

- **Highlights Summary**

  Spearheaded P&L management for operations units from $1.5M to over $200M. Key member of corporate leadership team that planned, executed, and sustained growth in revenues from $84M to $200M/year and increased profit 500% in less than five years.

  Managed the architecture, design, development, and implementation of intranet-based management information systems. Provided foundation CRM, ERP interfaces, financial performance, T&E collection for 1,200 employees, activity-based costing or services projects, and delivery resources valued at over $160M/year.

  Defined and implemented financial and administrative policies to support the development and startup of channel sales. Provided operations leadership and direction to sales, marketing, and product managers in support of "open systems" multi -tiered strategy targeted to grow from $0 to $24M in 18 months.

  Designed and integrated program frameworks that became the basis for $40M professional services business. Developed initial offerings to leverage world-class service resources in the areas of data center services, disaster recovery, data migration, and integration services.

  Generated and managed business charter and plans including: G&A expenses, capital assets, staffing requirements, operating and capital budgets, and forecasts for largest geographic service unit of a billion-dollar corporation.

- **Strategic Sourcing Compliance Management Resource Allocation Summary**

  Results-oriented analyst with extensive experience in procurement planning, process analysis/documentation monitoring, and policy procedure recommendation.

  Lead teams in development of best practices, such as strategic sourcing and implementation of long-term financial projections.

  Excel at developing new and improving current policy and procedures to gain operational efficiency and reduce costs.

Develop and document financial targets and business process tools to make breakthrough improvements in operational efficiency and impact fiscal policy

Create long-term contracts /strategies that are win-win solutions for all stakeholders.

Analyze new supplies and provide innovative negotiation strategies to meet competitive demand and build market share.

SOME TIPS ON HOW TO WRITE A SUMMARY OR A PROFILE

Open with your professional moniker—Production Manager, Sales Engineer, Corporate Trainer, Editorial Director, Web Designer, General Manager, etc.

From a format standpoint, it might help to bold and capitalize this designator. That will help you stand out visually right from the start—PRODUCTION MANAGER, CORPORATE TRAINER, EDITORIAL DIRECTOR, WEB DESIGNER, GENERAL MANAGER, etc.

Select your marketable skills from your previous assessments that link to the professional identity — with "five years' experience in high-tech manufacturing" (for the Production Manager) or "ten years of stand-up supervisory training delivery" (for the Corporate Trainer) or "seven years' writing and editing experience" (for the Editorial Director) or "four years' consumer agency expertise" (for the Web Designer) or "25 years' P & L responsibility in start-up and mature organizations" (for the General Manager).

You can sell yourself here even more with another descriptor sentence that includes your marketable, personal strengths. Look to the positive traits you have or to the consistent compliments you've received in performance evaluations or from team sports or volunteer assignments. Reflect on these skills that have gained you frequent kudos and recall favorable messages (including the praises of your family and friends), e.g., "clever problem-solver with two successful ISO certifications" or "exceptional writing skills with a strong background in program design and evaluation."

Exercise

A _____ with _____ in _____ and _____.

_____ with a unique skill set of _____,

and _____.

Some of the phrases below might help, as well:
- Broad range of experience in …
- Worked effectively in …
- A proven performer in …
- Extensive expertise in …
- Innovative
- Creative
- Committed
- Tenacious
- Additional training in …
- Attended
- Drove
- Grew
- Achieved
- Demonstrated
- Launched
- Captured

Prepare your Background Summary or Profile below:

_____
_____
_____
_____
_____
_____
_____
_____
_____
_____
_____

ROI (Recommendations, Opinions, and Insights)

Think English 101 in crafting your summary. Keep a parallel structure and your tenses consistent. (Remember also that even a company that ends in S is a singular noun and all modifiers must reflect this, e.g., "helped McDonalds reach its objectives" vs. "helped McDonalds reach their objectives."

Your summary profile is a good way to describe yourself and what you can do.

Memorizing it or being able to use it spontaneously will help you a lot. You can also change the header to reflect the particular position you are seeking, providing you keep a record of what you send for each job opening.

Have two or three clean copies of your resume and a good supply of business cards in each vehicle you own—carry supplies in a folio if you use public transportation—and be prepared to distribute them.

Strive for elegance in your choice of font, paper bond, and color.

✳ *Summary* ✳

✳ Knowing what you are good at and what you want to do is the beginning of building a resume that will bring results.

✳ Crafting the opening portions of this marketing tool often requires as much thought and care as providing the chronological or skill data presented later on.

✳ Consistency and good grammar count. Poor writing skills will always hinder you.

EXPERIENCE

Professional Experience or Experience/Accomplishments

This component or resume ingredient is perhaps the heart of your document, the opportunity you have to tell your buyer not only what you were responsible for but also what you were able to accomplish. This is your chance to distinguish yourself and to tell your story by responsibilities and by results. This is the most important part of the document you will use to market yourself.

Start by noting some of your accomplishments and achievements. Look at your accomplishments as another way of assessing your product worth to a prospective buyer. A list of your key accomplishments can be compiled from experiences at school, work, or home and reflect your various satisfactions and fulfillments. Craft statements that explain what you did and how you were successful.

You can also reflect on the skills that have gained you frequent compliments and recall favorable performance evaluations, including the praises of your family and friends (especially your new romance).

The point is that it's OK to appreciate your talents, get feedback from trusted opinions, and continue to tinker—not tamper—with your recipe for success. The more you understand about yourself as a product, what you can and cannot do, and the fluctuating demands of the job marketplace, the better salesperson you'll be for your skills and the better your resume will reflect who you are.

You might think of this list of your accomplishments as an "OAR" in the water, helping you row the boat of your resume to your destination.

O The opportunity. What opportunity was there for you? What was the problem? What was the context or situation at hand?

A The activity. What action did you take? How did you solve the problem and address the situation? What specifically did you do, recommend, or initiate?

R The result. What did you achieve? What was the successful outcome? What is the metric that quantifies your accomplishment?

Exercise

List four of your accomplishments considering the opportunity, activity, and result of each action noted. Choose accomplishments that are important to you and make you proud, events that made you feel satisfied and successful, activities that could be used in your resume. Explain them using the OAR format.

Sample Accomplishment Rating

Accomplishment: Increased the attendance at internal training programs

O   As a corporate trainer, I was chartered with improving the participation of internally sponsored programs.

A   Generated a first-time online needs assessment document and a follow-up brochure of topics linked to corporate goals.

R   Attendance increased by 68%.

Accomplishment: Identified "quick wins" for key distributions contracts

O   As a Contract Administrator, I was required to create a rebate program for contracts.

A   Negotiated an arrangement for distribution vendors.

R   Saved $90,000 in one quarter that led to $300,000 by contract expiration.

Accomplishment: Created five new ads in an eight-week time frame

O   As Director of Marketing Communications, I was chartered with integrating a new campaign style with current product/market launch initiatives.

A   Launched new ads in 90 days.

R   Received first place advertising award from the Biomedical Marketing Association three years in a row.

Accomplishment #1

O   _____

A   _____

R   _____

Accomplishment #2

    O _____

    A _____

    R _____

Accomplishment #3

    O _____

    A _____

    R _____

Accomplishment #4

    O _____

    A _____

    R _____

Next, it's time to take these OARs (Opportunity, Activity, Result) and begin to row. You need to polish these statements for use in this career history (professional experience) experience/accomplishments component of your resume. Create an employment history of who you are and where you have been successful.

FTE (Facts, Thoughts, and Examples)

We are all too often self-critical. For some people and in some cultures, looking to the positive is more difficult. To help focus on your accomplishments and personal strengths, revisit your past performance reviews. On what were you complimented? Where were you praised? Look for specifics and seek more than what your Mom would say if asked about your positive qualities.

First, consider each previous employment—what were your activities daily, weekly, monthly, and periodically?

Second, gauge the value you brought to your department and your organization. Third, focus on how you contributed to any significant changes.

Finally, note how you resolved these challenges. Where were you most successful?

Refer to your previous job descriptions

and performance reviews to refresh your memory for the role you played and the impact you made. See this as a "responsible for..., results were" exercise.

For the discriminate buyer, it's the results you achieved—the measurable accomplishments—which make the difference. It is also an ideal opportunity to include as many key words as you can to trigger scanning—and user—recognition. Check current employment ads for the latest terminology or words to include. There is no need to repeat terms.

To transform your accomplishment statements into your resume results:

- Keep it short and sweet
- Begin with verbs (e.g., managed, created, controlled, directed, etc.) and remember to check with synonym dictionaries to vary job descriptors (e.g., authorized—sanctioned, justified, warranted, allowed)
- Include the activity and the benefits of your efforts
- Whenever possible, use:
  Quantifiable metrics
  Key words in each statement

For example, some OAR statements that work well for a resume:

- Created an inventory control and recording system that improved department productivity by 24%.
- Attained a $62,000 monthly gross margin in first year.
- Drove company to increase its corporate product PR initiatives, increasing published PR by 60% within a year.
- Built a strong working relationship with Marketing to allow aggressive pursuit of configuration information ahead of project milestones—this increased manufacturing visibility, reduced engineering and materials issues, and consistently increased on-time delivery to near 100%.
- Managed global marketing communications efforts encompassing product launch promotional plans, advertising programs, exhibit planning, and Web marketing for a division, increasing annual revenues 25%.
- Upgraded 300 pages of marketing site sub; raised revenue 10% via subscription-free financial tutorial content.
- Created training materials to ensure smooth transition from one operating system to another, with minimum interruption in productivity. 5,000 employees were trained in one month.

Some action and key verbs that create attention:

Reduced turnover	Improved reliability
Expanded customer base	Designed new technique
Reduced cycle time	Increased productivity
Revamped …	Streamlined…
Turned around	

FTE (Facts, Thoughts, and Examples)

Some key words are especially attention grabbing—marshaled, championed, demonstrated, spearheaded—and when you post online, key words only appear once; there is no need to repeat them.

It's important to keep this part of your resume consistent, too. Use the past tense of action verbs to be most powerful—managed, led, developed, created, designed, etc. Remember, you can also include key words in a summary section (perhaps AREAS OF EXPERTISE or SPECIAL SKILLS or TALENT BANK—Tax Audit Supervision, Federal Excise Tax Collection, etc.).

Some metrics that generate discussion:

Increased sales by 20%

Reduced response time by 50%

Prevented $2-million customer from defecting

Reduced underutilization by 45%

Exercise

Read the examples below and then practice writing actions and results, using the sample presentation

ACTION TAKEN	RESULT
Crafted all form letters	Handled more than 40% of customer correspondence and negated need for additional staff
Conducted shipper audit	Corrected 135 original invoices and regained $65,000 in billing mistakes
_____	_____
_____	_____
_____	_____
_____	_____

Sample Presentation

AFFIRMAX, INC., SANTA CLARA, CA

Director, Marketing Communications, 2002-Present

Responsible for global marketing communications activities across multiple product groups. Developed advertising brand strategies, Web marketing initiatives, direct-mail campaigns, collateral, print/online media, and trade show programs. Also managed staff of eight, with budget responsibility of $3.5 million.

Results:

Managed promotional strategy and tactical communications plan for more than 20 product launches within a 12-month period.

Launched a new advertising campaign in 60 days, redirecting new campaign style with current products/market launch initiatives.

Received first-place advertising award from Biomedical Marketing Association three years in a row.

Built new exhibit property to increase corporate and product brand presence at exhibitions – card referral sheets increased by 15%.

LIFESCOPE, INC., MILLPOND, CA

Communications Consultant, 1999-2001

Responsible for managing communication initiative for the Hospital Business Unit, including product launch/exhibit campaigns, brand identity development, and Web marketing for nine Product/Marketing Managers.

Results:

Established first formalized marketing communications function for the Business Unit. Developed and executed comprehensive marketing communications plans to increase leadership image in the market – awareness studies showed 4% increase.

Identified product/program opportunities to support marketing objectives across two major divisions and led cross-functional commercialization team through the planning process to co-market, Met all time and all budget targets.

Launched first award-winning customer testimonial advertising campaign.

Now you can practice writing your own statements using the spaces below.

Company Name: _____ Location: _____

Position Title: _____ Dates: _____ (years only preferred)

Responsible for: _____

Results (or Accomplishments):

_____

_____

_____

Position Title: _____ Dates: _____ (years only preferred)

Responsible for: _____

Results (or Accomplishments):

_____

_____

_____

SOME QUESTIONS TO THINK ABOUT

Edit your employment history scrupulously, especially if you are a seasoned professional with many years in the workforce. If you want to include all of your previous jobs, there is adequate space, and your other work enriches the package or explains something potentially interesting or unique about you, consider creating a list titled like the one below:

Other Related Experience or Other Relevant Experience:

- Flight Attendant, US Air
- Desk Clerk, Trump Tower
- Ski Instructor, Incline Village
- Customer Service Manager, InfoWorld, Inc.
- Tour Guide, Wild River Adventure Experiences, Inc.

Dates of Employment

How Do You Display Your History?

Format-wise there are a few things you can do to draw positive attention. Be sure your dates of employment are easy to see and read. Keeping them at the right or left margin is probably the best.

Researchers have said that our eyes tend to look to the right, so if those employment dates run down the right-hand side of the page, you can't go wrong. Just be sure they aren't buried in the copy, that they stand out in some way. Because it's imperative to include your dates of employment (without them, too many questions and flags come up), you need to decide the best way to present them.

There is no real need to be overly specific either, even if your work history has been exemplary and linear. "July 9, 19 74 to June 19, 1977" is really no better than "7/9/74 – 6/19/77" or "July, 1974 to June, 1977." Perhaps the best and safest is to list by the years only: "1974 –1977." This is especially helpful if there are short employment stints, a variety of possibly embarrassing gaps, and numerous shifts in careers. No matter how you present the dates, always be prepared to answer questions related to your timeline no matter how you present the dates. Be consistent no matter what you choose to do.

Be mindful that honesty is always the best policy. The first things checked by reference checkers are the dates of employment, title, and salary.

Also, if all of your experience is with one company, be sure to highlight the tenure in bold "**1985-2005**," with the various positions held in regular type ("Vice President," 2003-2005) underneath and be prepared to underscore the periodic changes you managed and emphasize your varied expertise for any interviewer who may question your work range.

Again, if there are significant gaps in your job history (like that year you spent helping a charity or globetrotting for adventure?), be prepared to answer interviewer questions with a positive spin on your engagements, perhaps emphasizing volunteer work that tapped new skills or travel that increased your understanding of diversity, etc. If you were in drug rehab, incarcerated, or returned home to manage the household, skip any details and simply explain it as a maturing experience.

What About Titles?

A job title tells the reader what you were called and quite often what you did. You cannot make up your title—it needs to be an honest and accurate moniker and consistent with what the organization has on its records. Nevertheless, be sure you do not include something that is so internally specific that it could alienate or confuse the reader—Jr. Data Entry Clerk 111. Also be aware that certain companies create their own labels—Executive Administrator versus Executive Assistant versus Secretary or System Analysts versus Programmer.

FTE (Facts, Thoughts, and Examples)

Your resume can be the best icebreaker of all. Most people think they know what works and what doesn't … and … have experiences to validate their point. Ask them for some input. Use your resume as a way to engage or a way to get to know someone.

Look at your current role and choose a title that a reader or screener will understand and that accurately represents what you do. Attempts to make it fancier than it is or more important will backfire and get you into trouble.

The ladder progression for those who supervise others is often Manager, Director, Vice President, Senior Vice President, and Executive Vice President. Anyone who knows his or her stuff realizes that in a small company you may be doing the work but not carrying the title, yet you cannot claim to have the title if you don't.

If you work at a bank, for example, and have a VP title, it probably does not mean quite as much as if you were a VP at a Fortune 100 institution.

Sometimes your job title isn't an accurate reflection of what you really did. If not, then emphasize your responsibilities or focus on the function:

1) *Senior Secretary:* Coordinated the company's activities in five trade shows—designed and set up booths, created demonstration and scheduling, etc.
2) *Trade Show Coordinator:* Coordinated the company's activities in five trade shows—designed and set up booths, created demonstration and scheduling, etc.

DO NOT CHANGE YOUR JOB TITLE. Your company often provides this information to anyone who calls and falsification can be grounds for termination or a fast rejection.

What About the Company Name?

Always include the name of the company you worked for. The city and state are important to have, but not the street address or telephone number.

If the organization is an especially large one, including the division or even a brief descriptor will make it easier for the reader. Remember not to make the person reviewing your resume work too hard. Sometimes specifics help if you are changing fields or

> **FTE** (Facts, Thoughts, and Examples)
>
> Abbreviations are just fine here –Corp. for Corporation, Co. for Company, Ltd. for Limited, or Div. for Division. But once again, consistency is the key. It does not seem small-minded here, but shows caring and a positive attention to detail.

applying for jobs in other parts of the country. However, if space is a consideration, bank on curiosity to take hold, go for brevity, and wait to explain your organization in the interview.

Some Examples:

Embarcadero Publishing Company–Palo Alto Weekly	Palo Alto, CA
Spherion Corporation–Human Capital Consulting Group	Cupertino, CA
Johnson & Johnson–Lifescan, Inc.	Milpitas, CA
IBM–Computer Products Group	San Jose, CA
Gap, inc. Banana Republic Marketing Division	New York, NY
Monolithic Memories, Inc	Berkeley, CA
a manufacturer of diode electronics	
Ibank Corporation	Minneapolis, MN
an online commercial bank service	
Ematch and Over Incorporated	Dallas, TX
internet dating service for baby boomers	
Accuray Corporation	Sunnyvale, CA
manufacturers of radiosurgery robotic lasers	

Here's a sample that puts it all together:

PROFESSIONAL EXPERIENCE

MACMONSTER PUBLISHING CO., INC., 1990-2006
Telecommunications Manager - Business Division
Managed a telemarketing sales department of 23 for this $10 million company. Hired, trained, and motivated all staff. Collected market intelligence for product development. Established liaison with field sales personnel, customer service, and order-entry departments. Planned the acquisition of computer equipment to achieve state-of-the-art management information systems.

- Doubled renewal sales in six months.
- Recruited ten new sales professionals. All met or exceeded quota in the first year.
- Designed and administered all sales compensation and incentive programs, as well as performance measurements for individuals, groups, and product lines.
- Created departmental management reporting structure that provided vital market intelligence to other management groups.

EPSON MICROFILMS, 1984-1990
Sales Manager, Research Collections, 1987-1990
Managed sales of microfilm collections to major universities and government agencies. Recruited, trained, and managed personnel for inside and outside sales for this leader in the information industry with annual revenues of $80 million. Designed and administered compensation plans. Provided ongoing liaison with marketing and production managers. Represented business sector at trade shows and made site visits to major accounts.

- Exceeded forecast revenue by 10% and met expanded sales targets of $8 million.
- Conceived and executed all aspects of the first national sales meeting. Designed and conducted focus groups with customers for new product development.

Account Executive, Business Publishing, 1985-1987
Sold hardcopy, microfilm, and CD-ROM products to libraries and businesses. Executed market plan by computing past sales trends and projecting future isolated markets.

- Achieved 165%, 234% and 400% of sales targets in previously unproductive territory.
- Named Salesperson of the Year, 1986.
- Promoted into largest Eastern territory, with goals of $1,300,000. Exceeded sales goals.

Account Representative, Business Information, 1984-1985
Sold document delivery service to multinational accounts requiring published information on demand. Made site visits to approximately 35 Fortune 500 accounts. Represented product at trade

shows, state and national meetings and conferences.

- Number-one salesperson of eight responsible for launching this business sector, which is now well established in document delivery marketplace.
- Appointed to President's Task Force.

RESPONSIBILITIES AND ACCOMPLISHMENTS

WORLDWIDE BUSINESS AND TECHNICAL PUBLISHING, INC., New York, New York, 1990 to Present
An international publishing company serving the professional marketplace in the U.S. and Europe. Division of Worldwide Communications, P.L.C., a publishing and communications company with worldwide sales of over $2 billion.

Executive Vice President and Chief Operations Officer
Responsible for all corporate operations except editorial, human resources, and finance. Recruited to turn around this recently acquired, troubled, and unprofitable publishing business. Company returned to profitability this fiscal year.

- Revitalized the selling operation. In the most recent quarter, posted a 32% improvement over previous year results.
- ? Reduced operating budget by 20% including RIFs.
- ? Led the development and implementation of a package of new computer systems covering all aspects of the business from order-entry to financial reporting. Implementation to go "live" accomplished in seven months, a task that would normally require 18 months.

CENTRAL PUBLISHING, INC., Chicago, Illinois, 1984 to 1990
A $1 billion advertising, publishing, and marketing services company. The company operated in 29 states as well as internationally. It serviced 700,000 customers with over 400 products and services.

President, 1987 to 1990
Central Publishing Enterprises, Inc., Central Publishing International, Inc., and Central Yellow Pages, Inc., together accounting for $220 billion in revenue. Also responsible for the direction and development of $28 million of new ventures revenue, including directories, magazines, national sales, telemarketing, and international publishing.

- Improved operating margin by 42% while expanding product lines into profitable markets.
- Placed company's nontraditional and new ventures business under common supervision and provided direction to improve market penetration and profit.
- Directly participated in concessionary labor negotiations, resulting in $8 million in labor cost savings annually.
- Served as principal media spokesperson for the corporation.

Vice President, Sales and Marketing, 1984 to 1987

- Developed, led, and directed a new functional organization of 900 people with a $700 million revenue stream in four states.
- Improved revenue by 41% and gross margin on sales by 45%.
- Brought the company from last position in national sales in its industry to the number-one position. Led the country in sales for two successive years.

BABYBELL TECHNOLOGIES, INC., New York, New York, 1982 to 1984

Director, Computer Technologies Division, 1983 to 1984

Director, Planning and Administration, 1982 to 1983

CENTRAL BELL TELEPHONE COMPANY, Chicago, Illinois, 1978 to 1982
Assistant Vice President and General Manager, 1978 to 1982
Held several early career positions

SELECTED ACCOMPLISHMENTS:

GENERAL MANAGEMENT

- Developed specialty resin profit center that operated at capacity with a 40% ROI.
- Restructured an operation in response to changing market conditions, reducing staff by 8% and saving $2.7 million in operating expense. Stayed in the black while four competitors saw red ink and two failed.
- Effected a turnaround during a major recession by closing one plant, increasing capacity at another by 60% and doubling sales volume.

SALES/MARKETING

- Increased sales by 40% and market share from 29% to 33% during a period when the overall market declined 7%.
- Introduced national accounts program. Developed product line strategies. Coordinated promotional programs.

FINANCE

- Acquired two companies, one to extend market penetration and one to diversify the product line, and integrated them into existing operations.
- Oversaw the design and installation of a fully automated order-entry-inventory-billing system that interlinked 17 plants and 12 sales offices to improve customer service.

MANUFACTURING
- Expanded annual capacity of the chemical plant from 50 million to 85 million pounds.
- Managed the planning, design, and completion of a $15.5-million state-of-the-art manufacturing facility.

BUSINESS EXPERIENCE

INDEPENDENT CONSULTANT, 1991 - present
Independent Merger and Acquisition Consultant, working with companies involved in chemical and related industries.

BURNSIDE CORPORATION, 1988-1991
President and COO for wholly owned subsidiary of Seafox Planster headquartered in the U.K. with worldwide sales of $500 million. Responsible for all aspects of this building products company with 19 plants and 1,700 employees producing bricks, concrete blocks, and concrete pipe.

1985-1988
Corporate Vice President responsible for marketing planning corporate-wide and for general management of the Midwest Division.

1983-1985
Vice President and General Manager for the Midwest Division, which included two plants and serviced ten.

CENTRAL CHEMICAL CORPORATION, 1966-1983
Vice President (1975), General Manager (1969), Sales Manager (1967), Sales Representative (1966)
General Management responsibility for $40 million in sales. Brought in $7 million in profit. Managed sales, marketing, production, supply, distribution, and R&D. Additionally, managed sales and marketing efforts for $75 million in petroleum product.

ROI (Recommendations, Opinions, and Insights)

- Never, never, never alter the facts of your resume. Honesty is not only the best policy; it is the ONLY policy. Rejection and termination are the consequences of dishonesty. It isn't worth it.

- Inconsistency signals a slapdash approach and can turn off even the most big-picture, not-into-details person. Proofread over and over again.

- Make no assumptions that someone will know what you mean. Explain what you've done and how you've done it in the simplest of terms.

- If this component/section would make your resume three pages, limit your achievements to the past 10-12 years and include only the most noteworthy or particularly relevant.

✳ *Summary* ✳

Presenting what you have done is not enough. You must quantifiably explain the positive results of your work.

✳ Embracing the OAR concept will help you express your many accomplishments most effectively.

✳ Keeping consistent in writing and visual style signals the positive points of a concerned and thorough professional.

✳ Use strong verbs—"implemented," "generated," "created," etc.

✳ Use technical terms only if they enhance the description of your work. Avoid jargon—assume the reader does not know it.

✳ Use abbreviations cautiously and carefully.

✳ Use the third-person voice—avoid "I."

✳ Using action words and non-jargon industry phrases might attract positive attention from the computer scanner and show the human screener/reader that you know what you're doing.

EDUCATION AND PROFESSIONAL DEVELOPMENT

The chapter heading here should tell you a lot. Quite often, your education alone may not be enough for some employers. Many in today's competitive market are looking for people who are learning all the time, and who continue to gain knowledge after completing their formal education. They look positively on you if you distinguish yourself as eager to improve. It's also important to consider how much education and continuous learning are valued in your field of interest or industry. In some of the creative, more artistic fields, where and how much you studied are not always valued as significant. Just know that, in general, education can hold more importance if you attended a prestigious, recognizable institution and that telling your buyer that you have not only studied formally but also continued to take classes and learn your craft is an advantage.

FTE (Facts, Thoughts, and Examples)

Some human resource professionals claim that providing your major and minor subject areas makes it easier for them to sort and assess your resume. It may not make it easier for you, however, especially if you're a seasoned professional and your data is old and your work is unrelated now. Not including this level of detail should not keep you from getting called for an interview.

Where you place this educational information on your resume depends on your years in the workforce and your field of interest. If you're a recent graduate, if you're searching for your first career position, or if you have limited experience in the workforce, your education and academic achievements are major assets and best placed at the very beginning of your resume, right after your Summary Profile or Objective. They then become the first thing reviewed.

Remember that if you're a recent college graduate or new to the workforce, you should list your position on the debate team, your advertising sales record for the newspaper, club memberships, or special scholastic achievements.

Certainly your scholarship and awards need to be there, but including your major and minor fields of study might not be necessary.

Some research says that doing well in school is a positive indicator for doing well at work. Tell the screener anything you think that demonstrates your potential as a productive, value-added employee.

(The convention in some fields – medicine and law in particular—is to put your education and professional development in the beginning of your resume or C.V., as well.)

As your job experience and results grow, your academic credentials become less significant. Future employers care more about your work life and less and less about your school life. Then, you would put your Education/Professional Development at the back part of your resume, after your Experience/Accomplishments section. Begin with your highest degree; include your major, the name of your college or university, and its location.

List the highest level of attainment you are comfortable with. There is no need to emphasize a level of academic recognition that does not suit you. Plus, including the dates depends on your level of experience and if you are comfortable with your age being out there. After you have been in the workforce for 15 years or more, leaving them off is a better bet.

Start with the highest degree, even if you did not finish it. If, for example, you

left a Ph.D. program without completing your thesis, you can put ABD in the degree slot (all but dissertation). Or, you might be tempted to list your high school diploma first, followed by the university or college you attended but never finished. You do not want the situation to present you as a quitter or a college dropout. List what you studied and the university or college and location and never lie about completing a degree if you didn't. This lie is cause for instant termination or a fast rejection. Just leave your high school diploma off.

Remember to include that class you took in Public Speaking/Presentation Skills, the Seminar in Negotiation, or the Leadership Skills Program you were selected to be a Master Trainer for your division. (Even an EMT or special Red Cross Certification might be significant.) All relevant training and adult-learning experiences that relate to your goal should be listed and, if space permits, computer and software classes or special programming sessions, as well. Present the sponsoring organization as if it were a college or special school. Be proud of the time you spent and treat your development graphically as an integral part of your schooling, not an add-on.

Be sensitive to how the screener or first reader of your resume might react to your professional development. For example, the Human Potential Movement may have made you a better person and significantly changed your future, but including these life-altering experiences is more likely to generate negativity or discrimination rather than something positive or identifying. The 1970s were over 30 years ago, so leave off EST, Forum, Life Spring, Landmark, Mainstream, Actualizations, etc.

SOME QUESTIONS TO THINK ABOUT

What About Summer and Part-Time Employment?

Include this information only if you are new to the workforce or re-entering after an absence of many years. Places, times, and dates can indeed help the entry-level employee. The resume benefits if you downplay the part-time aspect, focus on the skills mastered, and use a functional resume format.

What About Languages?

Our world is now a global network and many organizations are looking to expand their client bases. Having a facility with languages could easily distinguish you. Include your level of mastery then – it can only sell you better. Once more, however, remember to present your skill accurately. It's acceptable to calibrate your expertise.

Fluent in French   Understand Arabic

Read and write Mandarin Chinese   Read Polish

Conversational Hungarian

What About Sororities and Fraternities?

Know your audience before including your participation. For a general distribution resume, leaving it off is a safer bet. (Times are changing; though mention of a fraternity or a sorority may signal a positive affinity for some people, it could raise a red flag for others.) If an interviewer wants to know or if it is an important data point, he or she will inquire when you meet in person. Better yet, if you notice the Kappa Kappa Gamma pin or spot the AEPi paddle when you are there, you can use it as an icebreaker or bring it up as a way to connect more personally with your interviewer. (See HIRE ME, INC.: Interviews That Get Offers, Entrepreneur Press, 2006.)

If you know that a certain firm looks favorably on particular fraternity alumni or your research shows Theta Chi on the President's Internet bio and you're a brother, then it's OK to list it on your tailored-to-order document.

What Do You Do About Abbreviations?

Though abbreviations can cause confusion and are not usually recommended for other parts of your resume, they are acceptable here. B.Sc., B.A., M.A, M.F.A., and M.B.A. work just fine.

This education and professional development section can also trigger future interview questions, so you need to be prepared with some answers.

What if You Didn't Go to College at All?
There is no need to apologize for not earning a formal degree. Respond non-defensively to the query and stress your experience and talents. Steer the conversation toward your accomplishments/successes and special skills.

> **FTE** (Facts, Thoughts, and Examples)
>
> Academic pedigree and educational credentials can be important (in some environments more than others) … but … lifelong learning and a willingness to study new things can distinguish you. Take the seminar, read the book, complete the tutorial, and visually feature the most relevant learning experiences proudly and prominently with any formal degree(s).

What if Your Education and Major Fields of Study Don't Relate to Your Current Position or the Job in Question?
Mention that your career plans have shifted significantly since your formal education, if an interviewer picks up on this mismatch. Explain that what you learned as a student has helped you in your career so far and goes well beyond your major field of study.

Examples

Below are some examples that illustrate some powerful, educational, professional, and developmental messages.

Sample #1 — for an Executive Director/Non-profit
EDUCATION/PROFESSIONAL DEVELOPMENT
Ph.D. – Counseling, George Washington University, Washington, DC, Harold Dunwoody Performance Award
M.A. – Counseling, George Washington University, Washington, DC
B.A. – Psychology, George Washington University, Washington, DC
Non-Profit Manager Certificate – Compass Point Consulting, Wilmington, DE
Business Development Seminar – Wilson Learning Corporation, Laredo, TX

Sample #2 — for a Startup Real Estate Investment
EDUCATION/PROFESSIONAL DEVELOPMENT
Ph.D. – Financial Economics, London School of Economics, London, England
M.S. – Finance, London School of Economics, London, England

M.A. – City Planning/Real Estate, Cornell University, Ithaca, N.Y

B.A. – Architecture, University of California/Berkeley, Berkeley, CA

State Scholar

Sloan Fellow – MIT Sloan School of Management, Cambridge, MA

Certificate – American Institute of Certified Planners (AICP), New York, NY

Certified Auditor – International Standards Organization (1SO 9000), New York, NY

International Realtor – National Association of Realtors (NAR), Boston, MA

Sample #3 — for an Associate Editor

EDUCATION/PROFESSIONAL DEVELOPMENT

M.A. – English Literature, Seton Hall University, South Orange, NJ

B.A. – English Literature , Kean College, Union, NJ

Advanced Editing Certificate – Writer's Workshop, San Francisco, CA

Web Design Seminar – QuarkXpress, Denver, CO

Sample #4 — for an Internal Coaching Position (Utility)

EDUCATION/PROFESSIONAL DEVELOPMENT

M.A. – Management, JFK University, Orinda, CA

B.S. – Communication arts, California State University - San Luis Obispo, CA

Coach Certificate Program – NLP and Coaching Institute, Santa Cruz, CA

Breakthrough to Success Seminar – NLP and Coaching Institute, Santa Cruz, CA

360 Profile Certificate Workshop – Personnel Decisions, Inc., Minneapolis, MN

Leadership Coaching Workshop – Right Management, Sunnyvale, CA

MBTI (Myers-Briggs) Certification – Otto Kroeger Association, Austin, TX

Sample #5 — for a Marketing Manager

EDUCATION/PROFESSIONAL DEVELOPMENT

Graduate Studies – University of Newcastle, Newcastle, UK

CRM and Performance Marketing Strategies

M.B.A. – Business Administration/Finance, University of Colorado, Boulder, CO

B.S. –Life Sciences, University of Illinois, Champaign/Urbana, ILL

Bulldog Marketing Seminar — Hewlett-Packard, Palo Alto, CA

English: Native; French: Professional; Spanish: Basic

Sample #6 — for an Engineering Manager

EDUCATION/PROFESSIONAL DEVELOPMENT

B.S. –Industrial Engineering, San Francisco State University, San Francisco, CA

Managing within the Law – AMA, Santa Clara, CA

Effective Communications and Presentations – AMA, Santa Clara, CA

Cross-Cultural Business Seminar—Chordia Software, Cupertino, CA

Sample #7—for Corporate Sales Position
EDUCATION/PROFESSIONAL DEVELOPMENT
B.S. –Business Management, University of Wisconsin, Madison, WI, 2004
Spin Selling Seminar – McGraw-Hill Corporation, New York, NY, 2001

Sample #8—for Corporate Field Operations Position
EDUCATION/PROFESSIONAL DEVELOPMENT
B.S. – Pre-Law and Political Science, Middle Tennessee State, Murfreesboro, TN, 1999
Global Commerce Certificate – California State University, San Marcos, CA, 2006

Sample #9—for First Professional Position
EDUCATION
B.A. – History, Carleton College, Northfield, MN, 2007 (Dean's List)
A.A. – General Studies, DeSalvo College, Minneapolis, MN, 2005
College Preparatory Degree – Midland High, Edina, MN, 2001

Sample #10—for First Professional Position
EDUCATION/TRAVEL/LANGUAGE
B.A. – Sociology, Wesleyan University, Middletown, CT, 2006
     Wesleyan's Dean's List
     Psi Chi, National Sociology Honor Society
     NFA/College Football Hall of Fame Scholar Athlete Award
Intensive Language Study – Instituto Internacional, Madrid, Spain, 2005
Fluent in Spanish and Portuguese; advanced beginner in French
Traveled solo throughout Western and Eastern Europe and Scandinavia, 2003
College Preparatory Degree – Andover Academy, Andover, MA, 2002
Andover Book Award for graduating senior displaying spirit, leadership, enthusiasm, and academic excellence

Exercise

Practice below with your personal data

Degree _____(Major)

Institution _____

Location _____(City, State) Year _____

Degree _____(Major)

Institution _____

Location _____(City, State) Year _____

Certification _____

Sponsoring Organization _____

Location _____(City, State) Year _____

Continuing Education:

Courses _____

Sponsoring Organization _____

Location _____(City, State) Year _____

ROI (Recommendations, Opinions, and Insights)

- Your education and professional development work can provide an instant connection with your interviewer. Be sure to do your research and try to discover where your interviewer went to school or what development activity(s) interest him or her the most so you can point out any link on your resume that applies.

- Deal honestly with your participation in any seminar. Treat it with the same integrity you would your academic studies. Attending two days of a week session is not the same as completing a seminar and getting the certificate and should not be presented that way.

- Be prepared to back up anything you put in this Education/Professional Development section. If you say you are fluent in Spanish and midway through your interview the discussion is no longer in English, you need to be able to hold your own. Not being able to continue might certainly end the process there and then.

✳ *Summary* ✳

- Putting your Education and Professional Development in the right place can set the tone of receptivity. A nonacademic professional in the workforce for many years who puts education at the beginning of the resume might signal lack of valuable or relevant experience.

- Acknowledging your interest in learning new things can only help distinguish you above the crowd.

- Embellishing *anything* about your education is too great a risk. The straight-arrow approach is the best one to take.

THE BIG "OTHER"

The data in this section should provide the reader with other important information about your "package." Include such things as technical or computer skills, licenses and accreditations, professional affiliations, civil service grade, military service, and publications and patents.

Sometimes it is not easy to integrate this information into the Experience/Accomplishments or Education/Professional Development sections of your document and they warrant a separate section.

FTE (Facts, Thoughts, and Examples)

Some organizations and particular interviewers have a positive bias toward non-profit volunteering and/or community involvement. If for some reason—work overload, family responsibilities, etc.—you really have no time or inclination, be prepared to explain why and be sure your answer does not make you seem self-absorbed or too "me" focused. It will not sit well long-term.

Present the information crisply. Be brief and to the point. For special skills, be sure you strengthen what you have described in your accomplishments and include technologies and abilities that are relevant to your job goal or career specialty.

For affiliations and memberships, keep them closely related to your work and field of interest. Most employers want to see if you are connected professionally. Some jobs, if you are higher on the ladder, or in a marketing, real estate, insurance, or sales role, require community involvement and connections beyond work. Then it's certainly acceptable and encouraged to include your membership in the Better Business Bureau, the Moose Lodge, Kiwanis, or Royal Society of Muckluckers. Your affiliations can signal an outgoing persona and a wide variety of networking contacts that could help the organization.

Include your work in charitable organizations and local politics. They can demonstrate strong organizational and interpersonal abilities and show someone willing to get involved in a cause or even someone caring/concerned beyond the ordinary.

If you have patents, in some fields potential employers will value your achievements and look upon them as a way to assess your professionalism. Articles and books carry weight in fields where public exposure of professional expertise is connected to getting ahead and patents are seen positively in key manufacturing and technology arenas.

For people in other fields, these successes are of minor importance. Be confident, however, that that they do tell the reader you are committed to your career and willing to

FTE (Facts, Thoughts, and Examples)

In some professions accreditation and licensure are musts, so be sure to include all the essentials. If you have yet to complete a "must-have," provide your status: Passed CPA examination October 2006 - Certification awarded June 2007; Passed CA Licensing Board Exam March 2006; Supervised hours complete July 2007.

put time and energy in establishing a reputation that could put you a cut above your competition. There is no need to include your publication copyright or ISBN number or that lengthy detail on your patent. Usually, it's sufficient to give the number of patents and the general areas.

For licenses and accreditations, make no assumptions. ("I wouldn't be applying if I didn't have that.") Mention every credential you have obtained in your field that you believe to be required or "convention."

If you have served in the military, it is OK to highlight your recognition and special assignments and tour of duty.

Questions to Think About

What About Written Testimonials or Third-Party (Personal) Endorsements?
Including either of these items puts you at great risk. Rather than set you apart, in the eyes of many, it could set you up as self-aggrandizing and full of yourself.

A one liner after a significant accomplishment could work—"Singled out as the best with over 120 day accounts." In general, though, these testimonials and endorsements are best for your files rather than your resume and are the kinds of documents to read when you're having a tough day of rejections or just need a boost. Moreover, if you are new to the workforce or are re-entering after years away, the content of these papers can be used to significantly enrich your resume.

> **FTE** (Facts, Thoughts, and Examples)
>
> Create an "atta-boy" file. Save a record of all the recognition letters and positive endorsements you have received over the years and read them when you need a boost or are feeling like your search will never have a happy ending. Keep a few gems available and ready to hand out just in case any one asks.

What About My Special Interests, Hobbies, and Activities?
There is no need to include any unique interests and hobbies. The risk of alienation outweighs the chance of a positive connection.

This advice is contrary to the advice given by many career professionals. Some resume experts recommend including these as a way to connect with your buyer's personal interests—say, as fellow adventure traveler and cordon bleu master chef. Nevertheless, your favorites may not mesh at all. These interests

Join an organization and get active in it. Or take a class that you've been postponin –something that will enrich your life, fulfill a fantasy, or make you more professionally marketable. Getting out and about will not only introduce you to people who might share your interests and hobbies (hereby increasing your network) but will also bring value to your package. Remember not to fake it. Join a church group only if you like church and study what really excites you and tells something about you.

could be polar opposites and might cause red flags or even trigger a negative bias. If you are that gourmet cook who loves to travel and are interviewing with a hiring manager whose spouse ran way with the Italian cooking school teacher, well, the mention of those interests on your resume will be creating an obstacle, and the chances of your getting the job go down. You also need to have some mystery in your package.

What About Availability and Reason for Leaving the Last Job?

There is no need to include this information. These topics are best left for a person-to-person interview or meeting. If you were not available, you wouldn't be involved in applying for jobs now. If you require a few extra weeks to finish a special project or complete an important task, you can talk about that once you've generated some interest in your package and sold your ability to do the job for which you're applying. If there are certain circumstances that you want to acknowledge, do so in a cover letter (see Chapter 7).

What About References?

It's not necessary to list names of references on your resume. In fact, it's unprofessional and a bit tacky. No one will check a reference before meeting you. If you must complete and sign the employment application as required — sometimes writing "see resume" and attaching the resume is enough — there are spaces for you to include names there. With most standard application forms, your signature gives the hiring manager or HR group the permission to call your references when the time is right.

Putting in the line "References available upon request" is unnecessary. At best, it may suggest "I'm clean. I've got nothing to hide," but it is readily understood that you can provide names of those who know you and your performance. If space is tight, adding that unnecessary line will also take up space that you need.

What About Graphics—Pictures, Charts, or Graphs?

The convention today is not to include your photograph, graphs of any kind, or charts. These items can detract from your "copy" rather than enhance it, and could clutter your document and distract the reader from your words. (Certainly, providing an attractive full-length photo if you're a model or the standard black-and-white "head shot" if you're an actor or in the media would be proper.) It's been many years since the right hand of the resume included a photo. It became clear that these photos took up space, told you nothing about an applicant's ability to perform satisfactorily in the position, and often generated bias of all kinds.

What About Personal Information?

There is no need to include things like your marital status, age, or overall health. (Things like parking tickets, softball league batting average, etc. are also superfluous.) Your goal is to get an interview; you need to present only the valuable information that will help make that happen.

What About Willingness to Relocate?

Including this information could create another risk. Avoid doing it. Once again, this is the kind of information that is best suited to talk about in an in-person interview (or even in that well-crafted cover letter). Even if you are planning to move to another community or to another part of the country at your own expense, there are costs to hiring someone outside of the local area. Relocation has "expense" written all over it, and if the market is robust, there is a built-in bias to hire from the local talent pool. Your goal is to get an interview; make sure that you don't present a possible barrier right upfront.

Examples: Below are some samples of items in the "other" category that work especially well.

SPECIAL SKILLS

- Proficient in Microsoft Word, Excel, and Access
- Network Protocols: Tcp//Ip; Novell Netware Ipx/Spx Http Sna (Ibm)
- Middleware and Database: Cognos Enterprise Reporting, Bea Weblogic, Oracle B1, SQL Server; Domino (Lotus)
- Proficient in Adobe Illustrator and QuarkXpress

LICENSES AND ACCREDITATIONS

- Certified Laboratory Technician
- RN – State of Michigan
- Minnesota Licensed MFCC

PUBLICATIONS AND PATENTS

- "Choreographing Careers," June, 1994, *Executive Excellence*
- "How Training Manager Become Corporate Heroes/Heroines," November 1981, *Training Magazine*
- *HIRE ME, INC.: Interviews That Get Offers*, Entrepreneur Media, October 2006
- US6118277 9/22/2000 "Magnetic detection of short circuit defects …"
- Eight other US. patents in electronics design and processing
- Authored/co-authored 77 research articles in archival literature, two books, and seven patents

PROFESSIONAL AFFILIATIONS

- Organization Development Network, Regional Vice President
- American Diabetes Association, Northeast Region, Fundraising Director
- Board Member – La Jolla Community Theatre – San Diego, CA
- Advisory Group – Life Sciences Information Technology (LSIT) Global Institute
- Advisory Board Member, Kidney Disease Outcome Quality Initiative, National Kidney Foundation

AWARDS

- Downbeat Corporate Quality Award for Release Management
- Downbeat Division Quality Award for Test Methods
- Flower Systems Corporate Quality Award
- Cleveland Newcastle Medal from the American Association for the Advancement of Science
- The Rx Club Award for Excellence in Advertising
- Exceptional Achievement Award, SRI International, 2004
- American Chemical Society Award of Excellence
- Scholar Athlete Award – National Football Foundation and College Hall of Fame

MILITARY

- U.S. Army Reserve, Lt. Colonel
- Retired - United States Marine Corps
- Six Years' Service United States Navy – 4 Polaris Patrol Awards

Exercise

SPECIAL SKILLS

_____

_____

_____

LICENSES AND ACCREDITATIONS

_____

_____

_____

PUBLICATIONS AND PATENTS

_____

_____

_____

PROFESSIONAL AFFILIATIONS

_____

_____

_____

AWARDS

_____

_____

_____

MILITARY

_____

_____

_____

ROI (Recommendations, Opinions, and Insights)

- Repeat – There is no need whatsoever to include any personal information or unique interests and hobbies.

- Remember, your goal is to get an interview. Including your availability or willingness to relocate on your resume will most likely prevent this from happening.

- A well-crafted resume can often be attached to that required and formal organization application – "See attached resume" – and can save you some completion time.

- Employers usually check references before creating and sending a letter offer or after making a verbal commitment.

- Be sure your references know about any change in your name since you worked together. If either your surname – due to a divorce or marriage – or your first name – due to a preference shift – is different, alert your network. If any of your references cannot instantly recognize your name, that failure could cost you the job.

- There is also a big risk of putting anything on your resume you are not prepared to explain or defend in an interview. Be mindful that anything on your piece of paper is subject to inquiry; you need to prepare your answers and present them professionally.

(See HIRE ME, INC.: Interviews That Get Offers)

✳ *Summary* ✳

✳ Including your career-related experiences and academic and professional development achievements will most likely enhance perceptions of who you really are and put you in a distinguishing and positive light.

✳ Being discreet and totally honest about what you include in this portion of your resume is a must. Preparing to discuss details of what is there and what is not there is bound to increase your chances of success in an interview.

PUTTING IT ALL TOGETHER

Polishing Points (for the Internet, Too)

Y ou have worked hard on all the important ingredients for your powerful resume, for the important marketing tool that will begin to present and sell your package to your interested customers. Now's your opportunity to build these components (from your efforts in the previous chapters) and put them all together.

Fill in your special data here.

My resume:

IDENTITY

Name: _____

Address: _____

City: _____ State: _____ ZIP: _____

Home Phone: (_____)_____

Mobile Phone: (_____)_____

E-Mail: _____

Objective (Optional): _____

_____

_____

_____

Qualifications Summary or Summary Profile: _____

_____

_____

_____

_____

_____

_____

EXPERIENCE/ACCOMPLISHMENTS

Organization: _____ Location: _____

Job Title: _____ Years: _____

Description: _____

_____

_____

_____

_____

Achievements: _____

_____

Organization: _____ Location: _____

Job Title: _____ Years: _____

Description: _____

_____

_____

_____

_____

Achievements: _____

_____

Organization: _____   Location: _____

Job Title: _____   Years: _____

Description: _____

_____

_____

_____

_____

Achievements: _____

_____

RECOGNITIONS/AWARDS/PUBLICATIONS

_____

_____

EDUCATION/PROFESSIONAL DEVELOPMENT

_____

_____

ADDITIONAL INFORMATION

_____

_____

SOME TIPS AND TECHNIQUES (POLISHING POINTS) WORTH REPEATING OR ELABORATING

a) In selecting your high-end, standard 8 1/2 x 11" paper stock (rag content bond)—white is often the best and most sensible; soft gray, cream/off-white, and light blue also work well—try to pick one where the water-mark is visible when you hold it to the light. This could create an "elegant" distinction.

b) In printing your copies on a letter-quality (laser) printer or professional photocopy machine, be sure to use black ink only and proof compulsively so there are no word breaks, smudge marks, or anything that could look like an imperfection in the print job.

c) In picking an easy-to-read typeface (Helvetica, Times Roman, or Palatino work well) and point size (12 point is preferred and easier to read for some seasoned professionals or those with strong corrective lenses), be sure you like them. You should use them in each of your marketing tools. You are striving for a consistency in look, with one advantage being that people are more likely to remember you.

d) In providing adequate white space and generous margins and in using bullet points and indentations to add emphasis, be sure you aren't being too cute or clever. You could highlight accomplishments (all **CAPS BOLD** works for headings and highlighting company names nicely), but using a lot of italics or underlines or exclamation points and/or mixing typefaces can be much too busy a look.

e) For a possible artistic differentiation in format design and to build on the notion that our eyes look to the right first, put your name close to the right margin, if possible, and align it with your years of employment. Place to the right margins whatever you want people to see first or remember most.

Here's a sample resume using this technique, but intentionally without accomplishments.

Sample Resume

(650) 326-5489	**ROY J. BLITZER**
618 Fulton Street, Palo Alto, CA 94301	Roy@RJBConsulting.biz

ORGANIZATIONAL EXPERIENCE

SPHERION CORPORATION   1998–present
Senior Director
Responsible for senior staff transition consulting, executive coaching, and team development activities for Silicon Valley practice.

HAGBERG CONSULTING GROUP   1996–1998
Senior Consultant
Responsible for providing organizational effectiveness consulting, executive development coaching and counseling (including 360 feedback, peak performance analysis, Myers-Briggs interpretations), and designing and delivering related management seminars and workshops.

ZENGER - MILLER   1979–1996
Vice President and Senior Executive Consultant
Responsible for implementing self-managing work teams and high-employee involvement/change activities to client organizations. Previous duties included directing the Professional Development Center, ZM's public seminar division devoted to professional advancement of human resource staff, sales, marketing, product development, implementation of instructor certification, and all internal human resource activities

AMDAHL CORPORATION   1979
Contract Consultant
Responsible for the creation and implementation of a corporate-wide attitude ("climate") survey program, including the development of related support materials, management information and development workshops, and employee feedback processes.

SYNTEX CORPORATION (now Roche Biosciences)   1976–1979
Manager, Training Development and Communications
Responsible for developing and administering training plans and procedures, conducting and supervising all programs for management and nonmanagement personnel, and coordinating and implementing career and organizational development activities. Duties also included supervision of employee education and communications.

TEACHING EXPERIENCE

UNIVERSITY OF SAN FRANCISCO, Adjunct Faculty – 1985–present
Graduate and Undergraduate courses in Organizational Behavior, Organizational Communication, Human Performance Technology, and Group Dynamics

UNIVERSITY OF PHOENIX, Adjunct Faculty – 1996–1998
Undergraduate courses in Organizational Management and Organizational Communication

MENLO COLLEGE, Adjunct Faculty – 1996 -present
Undergraduate Course in Management Practice

SAN JOSE STATE UNIVERSITY, Adjunct Faculty 1995 – Present
Undergraduate Course, Introduction to Business

FOOTHILL COMMUNITY COLLEGE, Adjunct Faculty – 1974–1989
Courses in Supervisory Management and Employee Communications

AFFILIATIONS AND ACTIVITIES

Human Relations Commission, City of Palo Alto (chair, 1997) – 1993–2002
Advisory Board, Institute for Social Responsibility (San Jose State University) – 1994
Advisory Board, Institute for Effective School Leadership (Packard Foundation) – 1986–1989
Member, American Society for Training and Development – 1983–present
Member, Organization Development Network – 1983–present
Ask "Dr. Business," cable sccess television show – 1993–present

PUBLICATIONS

Office Smarts: 252 Tips for Success in the Workplace, Globe Pequot Press – 1994
"Ask Dr. Business" column in The Tab and Palo Alto Weekly – 1994
Find the Bathrooms First with Jacquie Reynolds-Rush, Crisp Learning – 1998
HIRE ME, INC.: Package Yourself to Get Your Dream Job, Entrepreneur – 2006
HIRE ME, INC.: Interviews That Get Offers, Entrepreneur – 2006
HIRE ME, INC.: Resumes That Get Results, Entrepreneur – 2007

EDUCATION/PROFESSIONAL DEVELOPMENT

M.B.A., University of California, Berkeley
B.A., University of Massachusetts, Amherst
Certifications: Zenger-Miller
                    Skillscope
                    DiSC
                    MBTI
                    THE BIRKMAN

 R O I (Recommendations, Opinions, and Insights)

- Proof your resume extremely carefully to ensure that everything you want is there.

- Proof again to be sure your writing style, tense, choice of words, and grammar are consistent and reflective of who you are.

- Proof a third time for punctuation, typos, spelling, and formatting deficiencies. And, take another glance at the text to perhaps pick up something you've missed.

- Think about the value of changing the format rather than the text or copy. More than one version of your resume can cause confusion; more than one layout and/or format might increase response and results.

✸ *Summary* ✸

✳ Including all the components practiced—your contact information, a Summary Profile (a good opportunity for a Keywords piece), Experience/Accomplishments, Education/Professioal Development, and Other (publications, awards, associations) will most likely give you a complete and comprehensive picture of who you are.

✳ Using the Internet effectively can increase your exposure for interesting positions, yhet too much time in this are will hinder you getting out and meeting people who can help you.

CHAPTER

7

YOUR COVER LETTER

and Other Complementary Tools

Many career experts think your cover letter is equally as important as your resume. After all, it is often the first thing people see when you contact them, either by e-mail or by snail mail.

Your cover letter needs to connect with the right person, both physically and emotionally. It needs to hit the target the first time out. It needs to tell the reader that something terrific is coming, and then pull him or her into the experience.

FTE (Facts, Thoughts, and Examples)

Keep your cover letter to just one page. If it is any longer, it is likely to make the trash—if it is read at all—and you might seem everything from long-winded and egocentric to unorganized and even rebellious. Resume rules of paper size, color, and quality apply here, too, as does your choice of an easy-on-the-eyes typeface and font size.

It's the enriching companion piece.

There are several uses for your cover letter. Most commonly, you can use it to introduce yourself to a company, search firm, or recruiter, to respond to a print advertisement, to follow up a networking lead, or to reply to a posting on the Internet.

CREATING THE BEST

Stick with a layout and format that is business-letter traditional. A block, single-spaced design works best and should include:

- Your contact particulars or personal letterhead information
- Date (option #1)   Date (option #2)*
- Addressee's
  name, title
  company
  address
  city, state ZIP

- Salutation
- Body/Content
- Close
- Signature

For your addressee's name and title, be sure you have spelled it correctly and have the latest and most accurate title. A name can tell the reader that you have done some research homework or you do indeed have some connection.

* For your date, some prefer putting the date flush right rather than flush left with the rest of the information. This might provide you with a bit more space for your pitch and looks equally professional and attractive.

If you are unsure if Matt Tress is the Director or the Senior Director of Human Resources, play it safe and put Matt Tress, Human Resources. It's better to get it right, if you include the title. An inaccurate one could easily trigger some sensitivity or negative reaction.

For your salutation, try to use a name, not "Dear Sir or Madame" or "To Whom It May Concern." If you have met the person

> **FTE** (Facts, Thoughts, and Examples)
>
> In many ways, your cover letter follows a typical sales call. First, the salesperson makes a positive introduction and generates some interest. Then, he or she presents the product, sells to benefits, and stimulates a desire. Finally, he or she shifts the desire into action.

and/or know him or her from your research or networking contacts—say the Senior Director of Clinical Research at Genentech is Dr. Reuben J. (Jacob) Goodkin, but everyone who has had any contact with him calls him Jack—you might use Dear Jack and be OK. "Dear Dr. Goodkin" is still the safest and best. There is a fine line between pseudo familiarity and making a connection, and you should avoid crossing it.

For your body or content, do your best to create interest, attention, or quick recall. Your first sentence needs to bring the reader in, and the remainder of your information here needs to keep him or her there.

Get upfront and personal right off the bat, The best way to capture your reader here is to use in the very first sentence the name of someone who works at the organization or who knows your addressee. It needn't be a letterhead contact, someone important, someone you think has influence or power in the system. The research data says that any company employee or friend/acquaintance will most likely capture the reader's attention enough for him or her to read on. (Many senior staff in a job search will use a name only if they think that person can really have influence. This may prove a foolish assumption. The person who answers the front lobby phone might know the hiring manager or Senior VP more intimately than the Director.)

Use your network to get a name and check whether it's OK before you use it. (Distinguish, if you can, whether this person is a former colleague or someone your sister's roommate met on an airplane to Costa Rica.) Obviously, this will not apply to a pure cold call.

Be clear and direct. And be forceful about what you want. In years past, perhaps a line like "Piper Cubb suggested I contact you" might have done the trick. Nowadays, with competition so fierce and the number of candidates so great, the following might work better: "Piper Cubb suggested we meet" or "Piper Cubb thought we should talk about your opening."

Some sample first sentences for your body/content:

- Bob Cratchet, your regional VP and my next-door neighbor, wanted me to apply for your General Counsel opening.
- Sam Spade and I met at the Crosby restaurant last week, and he convinced me to call for an appointment.
- Holly Golightly and I roomed together at Amherst. Your name came up as someone I had to meet.

Some alternative opening sentences without a name:

- I've been researching the telecommunications industry, and IBEX keeps coming up as a respected organization that offers management training programs.
- The Web design field is changing almost as I compose, and I'm eager to bring my experience to you at Dearborn.
- The recent *Newsday* article (see attached) convinced me of two things: one, I want to make a contribution to your employee team, and two, I've got the qualifications and experience you are looking for.

For the remainder of this body/content section, try your best to match the *requirements* of the position with your *qualifications*. This "T Letter" or "echo letter" technique is easy to read and follow and should create that further desire. Your pitch here will have the most impact and trigger computer recognition if it repeats (verbatim, if possible) the key phrases that appear in the job posting or advertisement. When you match *requirements* to *qualifications* and *background*, you make it easier for the reader to see your able fit, whether it's a blind ad or an open ad. This style can increase resume readership and callbacks by as much as 30%, so use it.

Some samples of the T letter or echo style:

Sample Posting and Response #1 (A T/echo letter):

Job Posting

HUMAN RESOURCE PERSONNEL OFFICER

We are a large real estate brokerage looking for a Human Resource Personnel Officer with seven-plus years' experience in recruiting and hiring industry professionals. Must be familiar with the business, have administrative experience, and the ability to work collaboratively under pressure. BA/BS required. Reference #23465.

Response

I am responding to your April 2006, posting #23465 for a Human Resource Personnel Officer and am eager to talk to you about the partial list below and how your requirements match my qualifications:

Your Requirements	My Qualifications
Recruiting and hiring	Attracted and retained key talent with a turnover rate 50% below industry average
Direct administrative activities	Assisted manager in planning and executing all company HR programs
Real estate industry knowledge	CA real estate agent license
Seven years' experience	Eight years at G&G—three years as an agent
BA/BS required	BS Business Management

This looks like an exciting opportunity, and I hope to meet with you to discuss the additional accomplishments in my attached resume (i.e., the design and implementation of a company-wide training program that helped increase individual productivity) and how I can contribute to your success as well.

Regards,

Brenda Starr

Brenda Starr

Sample Posting and Response #2 (A T/echo letter):

Job Posting

WAREHOUSE SUPERVISOR

Customized food distribution corporation looking for a full-time Warehouse Supervisor. Excellent salary and benefits package provided. Applicants must be a self-starter, leader, willing to work night shift, and have three years' relevant experience. Degree preferred but not required. #505056

Response

Morgan Freedman
34 Shawshank Way • Milpitas, CA 94567
E-mail: mgf@hollywood.net • (408) 567-7893

Ms. T. Hanks
HIJ Distribution
7 Rebellion Place
San Jose, CA 95114

Dear Ms. Hanks:

David Bower of Gilroy Foods suggested I apply for your Warehouse Supervisor position, as advertised on Monster.com, March 28, 2006, posting #505056.

I have more than four years' experience in the consumable products industry and want to meet with you to talk about the match below:

Your Requirements	My Qualifications
Self-starter	Designed and implemented two warehouse programs
Leadership ability	Managed crew of four with 0% turnover
Willing to work nightshift	Led nightshift staff four years (prefer those hours)
Three years' relevant experience	Four years in industry
Degree preferred but not required	BS Operations Management

Chapter 7. Your Cover Letter and Other Complementary Tools

Sample Posting and Response #2, continued

I will call you next Thursday after lunch hour (1:30 p.m., PST) to schedule time to talk about not only what looks like an ideal job fit here but also the additional accomplishments noted on my attached resume, including the stacking and retrieval system I devised that reduced download speed 30%.

Feel free to call me at (408) 567-7893 if you have any questions. Thanks for your consideration.

Sincerely,

Morgan Freedman

SOME TIPS THAT MIGHT HELP

First highlight or underline the requirements stated in the posting. Then list them so you can easily see the matches. (Do this before you create the list to ensure including everything important.)

Limit yourself to five to six paragraphs and no more than one page. (You have about ten seconds to grab your reader's attention—that's about the same time it takes to buy a lottery ticket!)

Show your best ad jingle writer's creativity and grab the screener's interest with something enticing, such as: "I've developed some systems—I will share exclusively with you—that have produced a 12% gain in market capture and helped Dorky and Torky produce $3 million in revenue over the last nine months."

For those "cold" body/content sections (where there is no job description or nothing really to respond to), do your best to highlight your OARs (measurable accomplishments) or to position the kinds of problems you can solve or other things you can do to help the reader.

Some samples:

- I am writing because my skills are perfectly suited to help you launch your new ifax As product manager for the Papier1, I grew sales in my territory by 33%, brought in 15 new accounts, and won the "Rookie of the Year Award."
- I am a ten-year veteran Customer Service Manager. My experience and achievements include:
  Setting up a call center and reducing the complaints by 45%
  Retaining staff at 5% when the average turnover was 12%

- I'm eager to meet and talk with you about your staffing requirements and how my talents and abilities can help you meet your goals. I have:
Reduced yield in the production area by 12%
Chaired a cross-functional quality team that won the company-wide cost-saving award (our recommendation saved $650,000.00 in year one alone).

For your close, end on a positive note, proposing to arrange a meeting. Whet the appetite of the reader and make him or her want to call you in. Provide the information necessary to make it happen. Take the desire into action.

Some samples:

- I look forward to speaking to you about the results you can expect from me. I will call your office on Tuesday at 10:00 a.m. to answer any questions and learn when I can get on your calendar.

- I'm eager to talk to you about the information above and the other accomplishments in my attached resume. You can reach me at (650) 326-5489 to arrange an interview time.

- My paperwork only highlights what I can do—my interpersonal strengths and my ability to get things done come through only in an in-person meeting. I'll call about an interview the afternoon of the 25th, if I don't hear from you first.

- You can reach me at (650) 326-HIRE (4483) to arrange an interview. I look forward to it and meeting you.

For your signature, be sure to type your name and leave enough space for you to sign your name above it. Though it may be considered clever or even like a professor or physician to sign so that no one will be able to read your handwriting, take the high road and sign as clearly as you can.

"Sincerely" and "Yours truly" still rank as the safest closes, yet depending on a previous relationship or your own style "Regards," "Best Regards," "Warm Regards," and "Best Wishes" can work as well.

FTE (Facts, Thoughts, and Examples)

Remember that spellcheck is not foolproof and you need a backup system for your checking. Take a break between when you create that perfect cover letter and when you read it over and send it. Repeat—even the most minor error in grammar, spelling, or typography can do a huge amount of damage.

Sample Cover Letter for Recruiter Correspondence

Christine Keller
2902 Calle Glorietta • Tucson, AZ 85716
Christinek@profumo.net • (502) 346-7689

Ms. Robin Hood
Harper and Watson
688 Highland Circle
Tucson, AZ 85710

Dear Ms. Hood:

Option #1: John Monroe of Classical Health Group suggested I contact you. I am a senior operations/financial professional interested in an executive officer position.

or

Option #2: If you are searching for a senior operations/financial executive, I would be interested in meeting with you to explore how my skills and abilities may match your client's needs.

My expertise and skills include:
- Business Process Improvements
- Systems Integration
- Initial Public Offerings
- Mergers/Acquisitions/Divestitures
- Strategic Planning

I am committed to staying in the Tucson area. My total compensation requirement is in the $180,000 to $225,000 range.

Attached is my resume for your review. I'll call this week to see if we can meet and discuss the details of my professional experience.

I'm eager to be considered for relevant assignments and trust you will not share my paperwork until we have spoken.

Regards,

Christine Keller

Christin Keller

Enclosure

Sample Cover Letter to Answer an Advertisement

October 29, 200X

Human Resources Department
AMICO, Inc.
P.O. Box 7813
San Francisco, CA 94120

Subject: Human Resources Advertisement in October 27, 200X San Jose Mercury News

Since your ideal candidate will have two years of human resources experience, typing speed of 63 wpm, and the ability to perform detailed record-keeping and to work under time constraints, you will be interested in my background.

My two years each as a human resources records clerk and a statistical clerk for a large hospital have required performing accurate computation and interpretation of complex data under tight deadlines, which I have never missed.

As a new account interviewer for a retail store, I was able to explain the qualifications required for different credit limits to charge-account applicants without losing the good will of those who were less credit-worthy.

My typing was recently tested at 70 wpm.

I look forward to the opportunity to discuss how my background can meet the needs of your Human Resources Assistant position. Please call me at my home at (510) 555-1234.

Sincerely,

Sally Mander

Sally Mander

Enclosure

Sample Cover Letter to Employment Agency

56 Blank Lane
Harbor, FL 32617
June 15, 2006

Bob Sled
Sled and Sled Inc.
44 Ice Lane
Harbor, FL 32617

Dear Mr. Sled:

Enclosed is my resume for your consideration. I am an experienced secretary with strong word processing and spreadsheet skills, as well as the ability to handle busy phones and keep track of details.

I am looking for an Administrative Assistant or Secretary position in the greater Harbor area. My last salary was in the mid-$30s. My experience has been in the retail, manufacturing, and financial services industries.

As I have left my previous position due to a company-wide layoff, I am available immediately for new employment. I am asking that you do not send my resume to any organization without my permission. I look forward to hearing from you; I can be reached at (809) 123-4567 at any time.

Sincerely,

Claire Voyant

Claire Voyant

Enclosure

Sample Cover Letter for a Specific Company, No Specific Opening

456 Post Street
San Francisco, CA 94104

November 3, 2006

Lee Jones
Manager, Men's Shoes
The Walk Company
3033 Shattuck Avenue
Berkeley, CA 94702

Dear Lee Jones:

Chris Santos, an employee of your firm, has referred me to you. I am interested in discussing employment opportunities at The Walk Company.

I am an experienced office assistant with over 10 years of work experience. I am familiar with software programs such as Excel and Word Perfect 6.0. I have kept accurate inventory control records and handled ordering and shipping of stationery supplies. My employers have always found me to be enthusiastic and dependable.

Enclosed is my resume for your review. At your earliest convenience, I would like to meet with you to discuss employment opportunities that may be open now or may develop in the future. I will call you next week to see if we can set up a time to meet. Meanwhile, I can be reached at (415) 974-4848.

Thank you for your consideration.

Sincerely,

Pepper Salter

Pepper Salter

Enclosure

Sample Response Letter to a Job Board Posting

September 18, 2004

ICF Kaiser
P.O. Box 2608
Fairfax, VA 22031-1207
Attention: TW-CC2

Dear Sir or Madam:

I have seven years of software training and technical writing experience and am responding to your recent advertisement for a software trainer. Please allow me to highlight my qualifications as they relate to your stated requirements.

Your Requirements	My Experience
Develop, implement, and train employees	Developed, implemented, and trained employees to use Microsoft, Oracle, and internal software
Develop new training materials	Developed user guides, job aids, and practical exercises for software training
Assist IT call-center with application software support	Implemented and managed help desk for an internal software application
Three years' relevant experience	Seven years' relevant experience
Outstanding communication skills and strong writing skills	Attended San Jose State University's Professional and Technical Communication certification program

I believe this background provides the software training skills you require for this position. I look forward to hearing from you. Thank you for your consideration.

Sincerely,

Dinah Mite

Dinah Mite
Enclosure

Sample Response Letter to a Job Board Posting

Dear Hiring Manager and Recruiting Manager:

I am excited to be considered for the Business System Analyst V-SAP / APO position in Santa Clara Valley, CA.

I am a creative, visionary, and aspiring contributor with a strong background in marketing and operations, along with a keen understanding of how to plan strategically and align with the emerging technologies. These capabilities have been showcased and proven through my ability to use these skills across industries, including the semiconductor and workstation industries. I possess excellent communication, organization and presentation skills, which were best displayed through my interactions with both customers and partners internationaly.

My track record reveals that I have a rigorous work ethic that calls for meeting objectives, exceeding expectations, and being a team player while excelling in a multifaceted corporate environment. Upon request, I will happily provide professional and/or personal references.

Below is a partial list of my qualifications that match the requirements needed for the Business System Analyst V-SAP / APO position:

Position Requirements	My Qualifications
5+ years experience	7+ years experience
2 APO implementations	3 APO implementations
Detailed knowledge of Demand Planning	Extensive knowledge of Demand Planning

Along with this brief introduction is a copy of my resume. I look forward to talking with you about the information above and how I can contribute to this organization and collaborate in the ideal fit.

Thank you very much for your time.

Kind Regards,

Dick Tate

dtate@yahoo.com
408-628-7643

Sample Ad Response Letter

July 6, 200X

Mr. Karl David
Director of Administration
Pennsylvania Convention Center Authority
1101 Market Street, Suite 2820
Philadelphia, PA 19107
RE: Human Resources Manager

Dear Mr. David:

In response to your advertisement in the Philadelphia Enquirer, I am presenting my qualifications to match your stated job requirements:

Your Requirements	My Experience
"Experience in highly responsible administrative work"	Sixteen years of experience with demonstrated results in management and administration of high-impact human service programs, with five years' directing the development of human resource programs and policies in both public and private sectors.
"Experience in affirmative action programs"	As Director of Human Resources for the Private Industry Council, carried responsibility of E.E.O./A.A. compliance for the P.I.C. and for all subcontractors. In concert with the Philadelphia Futures Programs, developed working relationship that provided access to minority high school students to job and career opportunities available with the Philadelphia Stock Exchange and member firms.

I look forward to the opportunity to meet you in person to discuss how my skills and accomplishments can add value to the human resource management's role of the Authority. I will contact you shortly to see if we can arrange a meeting time at your convenience.

Sincerely,

Chris Anthemom

Chris Anthemom

Enclosure

Sample Letter to Retained Search Firm:

RICHARD H. TATE
233 Shearcreek Isle, Foster City, CA 94404
Home (650) 577-1234, Office (408) 255-3992
e-mail: Dicktate@msn.com

December 9, 200X

Mr. John Wheadon, V.P. Development
Pacific Inxight
3400 Hillview Avenue, Building I
Palo Alto, CA 94304

Dear Mr. Wheadon:

Roy Blitzer suggested you might have an interest in my background in connection with a CEO position you are trying to fill. Please call me so that I can learn from you whether you have any portfolio companies where I may help. I will appreciate whatever time you can give me. Attached is a summary of my accomplishments and biography.

Sincerely,

Dick H. Tate

Richard (Dick) H. Tate
bcc: Roy Blitzer

Write your letter here. Your contact particulars or personal letterhead information, the date, addressee's name, title, company, address, salutation, body/content, close, and signature.

_____

_____

_____

_____

_____,

_____

_____

_____

_____

_____

_____

_____

_____,

OTHER TOOLS THAT COMPLEMENT YOUR RESUME

Business Cards

Remember that your cover letter is just one other marketing tool you have at your disposal.

If you're no longer working (and are without a company business card), it's important to create one. Generate a card that reflects who you are or who you want to be. Keep this card handy at all times and use it often, handing it out at networking events, including it with correspondence, and more. If you meet someone at a formal networking event or at a dinner party or on a weekend holiday, make it a point to hand him or her this new business card. Deliver a card that states your marketing message clearly and that will declare your specialty. Often, this card is best as your first contact follow-up. Your resume follows.

If possible, design the card in keeping with the "brand identity" of your other marketing materials, so you present an organized, cohesive, sure image. If you prefer an off-white or cream paper for your resume and stationery and a block typeface, use a coordinating color and type for your business card.

Local and national copy centers and large office supply chains offer business cards at reasonable prices (200 one-sided pieces for about $15). There are also Web sites that will print your cards for free, with colorful designs and a variety of options — but they also include their company info on the card's reverse side, advertising their benefits as well as yours. Some may see your card, then, as a frugal venture (maybe those hiring a budding accountant) and others as a cheap shortcut (perhaps those hiring a creative graphic artist).

It's fun to create your own card, but it can be challenging, too. You want to put your career story in sharp focus; using about 12-15 words on a small card. (If you have two or three legitimate skill sets to share, you can put a bulleted list of them on the back of the card, too.)

And the artwork says much about you as well. Block type says orderly; elegant type says creative; crayon type, says... well, let's not go there. Any additional color background, texture, and/or pictures all convey your message. But don't overdo the artwork (you'll appear indulgent) or try too hard to make it capture "the whole you." (It's a blurb not a birth certificate!) If you're looking for work as a charter boat captain, it's OK to use a picture of a fishing boat. If you work in computer programming, the "mouse" photo on your card is fine. The business card is for gaining business, not telling the world about your favorite hobby. There are cases where a clever card can win you attention and lasting recognition (as many boring cards get tossed and forgotten). A professional woodworker at a building products trade show even offered business cards made from thin slips of real wood — now that's class!

Check out some samples below.

FTE (Facts, Thoughts, and Examples)

Treat yourself to a distinctive calling card holder—a real leather one or a clasped, brushed metal piece. Go the extra mile and ensure that your card will be clean and not dog-eared. Even in presenting it, you could create a classy impression. Accessories might make a difference.

Sample Business Cards

PENNY CILLAN

Immunologist

303 Helpful Avenue   (650) 424-4000
Biotech, CA 94104   penny@cillan.net

BLANCHE DUBOIS

MANAGEMENT ENGINEERING

For Improved Productivity, Quality, and Safety

3661 Williams Way   Days 607-239-6023
New Orleans, LA 56709   Eves 512-689-5600

Bdubois@gentlemancaller.com

Sample Business Cards, continued

IGOR VRONSKY, PH.D.

Strategic Alliance • Technical Marketing
Business Development • Technology Consulting

(408) 356-0695 • Fax: (408) 356-0694

E-mail: ivronsky@tolstoy.com

14278 Novel Lane • King of Prussia, PA 60689

IVA LIVER

210 Liquor Lane   Tel: (312) 888-8900

Mead, Illinois 30303   Fax: (312) 888-8901

ivaliver@abuse.com

HAROLD ("HOP") A. CASSIDY

Engineering & Project Management

725 Cowboy Way   HACassidy@whitehorse.com

Hollywood, Florida 914007   Phone: (213) 654-5407

Fax: (213) 654-5408

Experience with development and manufacture of

- Specialty Chemicals & Materials
- Drug Substances & Pharmaceutical Dosage Forms
- Disposable & Consumable Devices/Supplies
- Electronics Components

Sample Business Cards, continued

LOIS LANE

Sales and Business
Development Manager
2209 Superman Drive
Smallville, IA 70906
Mobile: 739.323.0609
Fax: 730.423.0608
ll@clarkkent.biz

Unique accomplishments include:
+ Opened 12 new key accounts in first year
+ Broke two records for highest weekly billings ($300 & $400 K)
+ Developed and closed contracts with average markup of 50–70 percent
+ Won Performance of Excellence award 2001–2006

CD-ROM BIOS: PICTURING YOUR SUCCESS STORY

You can use Internet technology to generate a CD-ROM biography as a supplementary tool for your resume and to mention in a cover letter. You can take advantage of the Internet beyond tapping job posting sites, crafting e-newsletters or blogs, and mounting e-mail campaigns. You can build your bio on a CD-ROM. This can be as valuable and practical as a paper business card or resume and enable you to compete with the increasing number of job seekers who are upgrading their contact info to include the benefits of the CD medium. (See *HIRE ME, INC.: Package Yourself to Get Your Dream Job*, Entrepreneur Media, 2006, Chapter 5, for overall Internet suggestions.)

A CD bio, while slightly more expensive to make and distribute than the paper versions, and therefore best shared only with those in your primary target group, offers a unique way to showcase qualifications and distinguish your credentials from competitors.

Including many of the presentation advantages of an e-newsletter, the CD bio also allows you to control how your material is displayed but with greater amounts of content and handy portability.

For example, you can transfer content files (nonproprietary material and/or with written permission from the publishers) from various computers as dozens of images and text files. These may be loaded onto a CD as images of your activities with job presentations, community contributions, nonprofit work, and professional speaking engagements, or as texts of your business forms, tables, white papers, performance awards, recognition articles, PowerPoint presentations, intranet announcements, and organization charts highlighting your career accomplishments.

The CD bio also makes a great item to hand out at networking events, provide in an interview as a "sales" demo, or include in a mailer. Also, unlike material sent electronically, is less likely to be tampered with, corrupted, or deleted in the transmission process.

Once you have burned these files onto a CD, you have the further ability to catalog, store and save, and arrange the reams of documents for easy "at a click" user review. (By comparison, accessing the same info through an e-newsletter might take many extra page views or through an e-mail might take considerable time to download; and in each case a user's computer might not be able to handle opening the larger-megabyte attachments.)

ROI (Recommendations, Opinions, and Insights)

- Remember to fashion your cover letter as a "T" or "Echo" letter, if at all possible (when you have a job description or an Internet posting, especially)—Your Requirements matched to My Qualifications. After your opening paragraph comments, list in the left column several key requirements as identified by the job posting and in the right column the skills and/or accomplishments you have that match these. This way you can show how you are the candidate best aligned to the job needs.

- Take heed that except for the high-end executive search firms, there's no need to include your salary requirements or salary history in your initial cover letter. Focus on the key phrases that will catch attention and generate a call to interview. Money talk is best left to later in the process.

- Use the Internet –and the company's site in particular– to gather information to include in your cover letter. Reading this info about a company on its site not only helps you determine how to compose your cover letter to emphasize your fit with their need but also is knowledge you can use (if you study it well and have the facts straight) to drop into key points during an interview.

✻ *Summary* ✻

- Spending quality time crafting a powerful cover letter or designing a distinctive business card (when you are not currently employed) is energy well spent. All too often your resume does not stand alone.

- Thinking of your cover letter as a journalistic exercise—with answers to What, Where, Why, When, and How (you can help the organization)—will ensure you are selling your basics.

- Creating those Internet tools to supplement your resume, cover letter, etc., can indeed distinguish you ... but quality and professionalism must be "top of mind" or you will be remembered for the wrong reasons!

- Remembering the low response rate for cold Internet posting and mass company mailings should help you keep your perspective. Don't spend a lot of time at your computer or snail mailing to organizations.

CHAPTER

8

SPECIAL INTERNET TIPS, HINTS, AND POLISHING POINTS

oday's clever marketer knows how to use the Internet, and you will be left behind if you do not consider the Web as an integral part of your search and as a way to expose and distribute the computer-friendly resume you are building.

See *Chapter 5 in HIRE ME, INC.: Package Yourself to Get Your Dream Job* for details on integrating the Internet into your strategy. You should know that it is best for communicating instantly, conducting research and gathering information (especially when you are relocating or sleuthing company data), posting your resume, and e-mailing it.

Just be mindful that too much time on the Internet can take you away from networking and other approaches that bring significantly better results.

USING A RESUME BANK

Most capable job-posting sites include a resume bank. You can store as many as five resumes (and cover letters) at one time. Assign them unique titles for different applications. Then, when a posting appears on the base site (or any other), you can simply upload your resume targeting the job title or description.

Now, some career coaches, with good reason, warn you not to distribute more than one version of your resume, fearing that two differing versions of your resume might wind up on the same hiring manager's desk, which can be embarrassing and kill your job chances.

So "multiple resumes" here means documents that emphasize different aspects of your skill set. For example, say you have an equal balance of both magazine and Web site editing experience. If two job postings appear asking for an editor of either just magazines or just Web sites, you can choose to send the version of your resume that highlights your print or your Web skills. Either resume is equally accurate, but you have marketed your skill sets to different targets, increasing the chances that the recipient of your resume will read it with interest.

A resume bank can also log "hits" on your resume. You can select a program that allows various readers—recruiters, hiring managers, companies, other job seekers—to view your resume as posted on the site. Each time someone opens the link to your resume, you receive a hit and are notified what type of reader viewed your page. This info can be helpful to track which of the five resumes in your bank gets the most attention and from whom, allowing you to perhaps refine and model the others to catch similar interest.

Some resume banks indicate that your resume will "expire" after a set number of days—from 30 to 90 days—meaning it will disappear from view, so you'll have to upload or simply refresh it often. Even in the best banks, your resume can be "pushed down" to the bottom of the resume postings list, so a reader may have to scroll down several pages or more to see your entry, as the site keeps adding resumes from your peers. The best approach is to check on your resume listing every week or two, go into the bank, and refresh the resume (simply changing a word in the title or rearranging items) so you can post it again and the site will read it as "new" and display it atop the listings.

FINDING THE OPPORTUNITIES

Just keep in mind that the Internet job resource, like even the best, most-seasoned career advisors, can only point out job search techniques and opportunities—it's up to you to track down and capture the job.

If there's one aspect about the Web that's a given, it's that there's at least one job search site offering the perfect position for you.

The trick, of course, is how to find it. (And the fervent search can be a little like clicking through matchmaker sites to find your best "mate"—knowing all it takes is the right one to make you happy.) There are plenty of search engines hoping you'll give them a try.

> **FTE** (Facts, Thoughts, and Examples)
>
> Check for openings on the Internet first and then lean on your network to see if someone has a contact name there. Dash off an e-mail or make a few phone calls there before responding. That way you can use a name in your cover letter reply.

You can Google it. Or Excite yourself. Maybe Ask Jeeves or hear it from Mamma. Let it roll with Lycos or start slowly with MetaCrawler. Get the Big picture or enjoy the AltaVista. There are plenty of diving points into the Internet's tide of job opportunities—you just have to go for it.

Keyword Search

You can streamline your search to make the task a bit easier and faster. That means knowing important keywords to locate precisely the online job info you seek.

Many of your keywords will derive from your targeted job title. Try inputting several variations. For example, if you are looking for job sites catering to Web design professionals, you might enter:

- Web designer
- Web developer
- Web artist

- Web programmer
- Web graphics

or any combination of the above, including phrases such as:

- Web page design concepts for B2B (or B2C) sites
- HTML coding for Web design projects
- Navigation protocols for Web designers

(More about key words for your resume later on in this chapter, but for more detailed Internet counsel, see *HIRE ME, INC.: Package Yourself to Get Your Dream Job*, Chapter 5.)

Another way to use job search engines effectively is to collect all the entries you have clicked on and bookmark each to save them in a folder for future reference—perhaps even create several folders labeled by search engine or sites. That way you can quickly locate a search engine and, if applicable, use the search engine's log of your previous entries so you can pick up from the point where you left off.

Search Engines

Many job seekers have found the mega search engines a big distraction after a while. Certainly the search for appropriate and purposeful job posting sites is critical, but you should initially select up to a dozen key job sites. Perusing new links beyond those selected sites can tease you away from your main search into pursuing sites with job-related products (resume preparations) or services (bulk e-mailing) or just pure entertainment (famous bad job applications).

Not to remind you of this again, but … fewer than 10% of jobs filled are landed through the Internet. So it's great to use the Web to research jobs that pay, but not to linger on sites for play.

> **FTE** (Facts, Thoughts, and Examples)
>
> One note of caution: Do not become overly dependent on a search engine. Try not to spend too much time "just looking." For one thing, after about the first eight to ten pages of entries listed, the value of the entries falls off greatly. The search starts to turn up fewer and fewer appropriate matches, although you may still find job board ads placed on the right navigation column of some pages helpful the deeper you mine the category.

Of course perusing job postings—every day!—is the main reason anyone visits a job board site (though many such sites offer additional services, as discussed). But merely scanning line after line of job titles—and some titles can be laughingly irrelevant on less effective search sites—won't help.

Let's say you go to Jobs.com (yes, there really is a *www.jobs.com*—the site originators were obviously quick to grab that URL) and you type in "Software Marketing Manager." Now the pages deliver 100 or so job postings covering that title or a close variation. Wow, you think, this is going to be easy pickings. The numbers are surely on your side. Just click on one posting after another, e-mail a resume to the poster's address, and if even just 10% of the posters reply you'll have your pick of ten interview invitations, right?

Well, not so fast. You cannot count too much on bombarding job listings with a mass mailing campaign. (See *HIRE ME, INC.: Package Yourself to Get Your Dream Job*, Chapter 2.) Remember, it's all about your precision marketing to qualified target organizations. Just because mass mailing via the Internet is five times faster, reaches far more recipients, and, in most cases, is free, the results (sorry to report) are not proportionately much better. And keep in mind that others are thinking the same as you about the ease of applying for jobs on the Internet, which means potentially tens of thousands of competitors around the region and country—or even the world!

Sending reams of your resume into the "Black Hole" (you know, that place where all good unsolicited resumes go to die), whether as hardcopy or softcopy, is folly.

Click on the links, read each listing carefully, and keep copies of the postings that interest you. Learn from them before jumping ahead with your application. See how different companies in your field describe their open positions. Consider these aspects:

- How are the descriptions similar? Different?
- What is the tone? (Some postings want to screen out casual job seekers, so their copy can be downright intimidating or sound like a warning— "We work extra long hours and love it; so if you like to leave at 5:00, don't bother to apply!")
- Which postings indicate a salary?

- Which explain the job thoroughly?
- Which offer a company history or mission statement?
- Which cite their customer base?
- Which ask for references?
- Which list job goals, responsibilities, and qualifications?
- Which note any "definite plus" skills desired?
- Which require a job test or work sample?
- Which do not include a company name or address? (Watch out for these listings: some recruiters, HR managers, or even job seekers in your field, post fake jobs just to see what talent will apply.)
- Which indicate when the job opening will be closed?
- Avoid including any personal information about your race, marital status, religious or political affiliations, etc.
- Avoid including your references or stating "References Available Upon Request."
- Avoid providing your salary expectations and history.
- Present only the truth—be honest about everything or be prepared for an immediate termination if any falsehood is discovered.
- Stick to two pages; use a third for extensive publication lists.

You need to distinguish not only the job titles that match your needs but the specific responsibilities. And note that many new jobs within a company (especially a start-up opportunity) are subject to changes in the job description and its tasks—even as soon as the first week after the vacancy is filled!

Here are some popular mainstream job posting sites you may find helpful (a discussion of industry and career-specific job posting sites):

- BigEmployment.com
- CareerBuilder.com
- CareerMarketplace.com
- Craigslist.com
- EmploymentGuide.com
- Employment911.com

FTE (Facts, Thoughts, and Examples)

Any document you create for Internet use—resume, newsletter, personal Web site, blog, CD-ROM, bios—needs to be of the highest caliber possible and as professional as you can make it. Using an amateurish and/or hokey piece will do much more damage than not having anything. Some senior staff hire a creative specialist to create these items. Test whatever you generate with colleagues for honest input.

- HotJobs.yahoo.com
- JobBank.com
- JobCentral.com
- JobFactory.com
- Monster.com
- 6FigureJobs.com
- USAJobLink.com

The obvious strength of generalized job posting sites is their sheer reach and volume of coverage. But the best search is often the one most refined (or "getting granular" in your data mining, as Webbies like to say).

You can go from using a job search engine like Google that yields hundreds of pages of results to a generic job-posting site such as CareerBuilder for scores of pages to a career-specific job board such as Dice.com (for the tech industry) to see dozens of offerings.

It may seem like you're limiting your options by digging this deep but you're also hitting pay dirt in finding the most jobs with which you are the most familiar and that you are most likely to land.

Career Specialty Job Boards Worth Checking Out

Niche job boards are as numerous as there are job types. Beyond QuintJobs.com, a portal or gateway site to lists of career-specific job boards, here are a few in various career areas:

- ih200.net (law enforcement)
- k12jobs.com (teaching)
- marketingjobs.com (marketing)
- nationjobs.com/medical (healthcare)
- salesjobs.com (sales)
- financial-jobs.com (financial)
- writejobs.com (writing)
- fashion-jobs.biz (fashion)

Once you identify a job board that suits your career interests, you can tap many of the offerings and tools as noted above for more generalized sites, with a few very key unique provisions as well.

Many of these sites include the following features:

- *Career newsletters*—articles with trade news, executive profiles and job leads

- *Blogs*—user-supplied topics (and sometimes just outright gossip) that are invaluable for learning how your peers have fared in their jobs or what they think about contacts at specific companies where you may be applying

- *Employer job postings*—including some of the "hidden jobs" that are displayed here because they are composed in a job's particular jargon, extra-fine task detail, require unique expertise, or are targeted to industry-only applicants

- *Company announcements*—links to sites of companies known to be undergoing mergers, acquisitions, new product developments, reorganizations, relocations, new branch or division set-ups, etc., that note transitions and changes that may lead to fresh job openings

- *Part-time or flexible work options*—listings of opportunities other than full-time salaried jobs, including freelance assignments, investment aims, internships, training, or start-ups

Another advantage of niche job boards similar in intent to discussion boards is the "peer-group job search." Once you sign on here, the commitment is more exceptional. You can join online groups of as few as five members or as many as 25, but in any case, the plan is to work with your virtual peers to find jobs for one another. (If you've ever played online poker with virtual competitors or shopped Web auctions with other bargain hunters, you have an idea of the communal approach to getting what you want from the Internet.)

FTE (Facts, Thoughts, and Examples)

If you choose to post your resume on a job board, be sure to find a few keywords that you can religiously change every week or every other week. Most sites refresh and move new resumes to the top. Even that one word shift will bring your paperwork forward.

Company Job Boards

Sometimes, and this seems obvious, it's best to go right to the source. In the offline world, this might take the form of walking into a company's lobby and handing the receptionist your resume addressed directly to a hiring manager you know. On the Web this means logging onto the site of a company in your target group, checking its job postings, and e-mailing your resume to the firm's specific employment code—or possibly e-mailing a resume to a company contact you met through networking who directed you to the site to apply.

The value of applying to a job description posted on a company site is at least threefold:

1) You can assume that the posting is credible.

2) The job is clearly recent, relevant, and likely still available.

3) It is presented in the context of the company's corporate organizational structure and/or current employee needs.

Another advantage of dealing directly with a company site in applying online for a job is that you can readily see the firm's industry standing, mission, brand messaging, PR announcements, latest products and/or services, awards and distinctions, stock status, history, employee count, branches, affiliations, corporate and board officers' background, and more.

> FTE (Facts, Thoughts, and Examples)
>
> Some company Web sites might not be as polished as you'd expect. At this stage, keep an open mind and remember not to write off the position because the site, job description, or "whatever" does not meet your standards or expectations. The reverse is also possible. The company with the fantastically creative site and clever description and materials could be a jungle.

ONLINE FILE FORMAT

There are two computer-compatible (soft copy) formats to try, even if you ultimately choose not to post your resume online.

ASCII

This is an unformatted version, without underlines, bolds, bullet points, etc., and is the most commonly understood by any computer regardless of the software or platform used to generate it. It is much easier to use as an attachment or copied into the body of an e-mail. Instructions for converting your resume to ASCII are:

- Open resume in MS Word.
- Under "File," choose "Page Setup" and then "Margins." Change margins to reflect one inch (top, bottom, and sides). In page Set Up, delete headers and footers. Then "select" the entire document, left justify, unbold any words and select Courier 12 point for the font.
- Choose "File" and "Save As" and then, for "Save as type," choose "text only with breaks." Disregard warning that sometimes formatting may be lost. Exit Word.
- Open your resume in Notepad (a software program usually bundled with Microsoft Windows) by going to Desktop, click "Start," "Programs," "Accessories," "Notepad."
- In Notepad, select "File" and "Open" (your document will have a ".txt" extension).
- ASCII documents should contain characters (i.e., %, &, bullet points, etc.). Use space between paragraphs and sections of text for emphasis.

HTML or Web

This is a formatted version that permits hardcopy options (bullet points, bold, italics, etc.) and is an increasingly popular way to showcase your accomplishments and achievements by linking your resume with Web sites. It is a way to market yourself online. This version can, however, be time-consuming to generate and may include everything from just a Web page equivalent of your word-processed document (with some links, too) to several pages with an index and links to different resume sections. Consult with a Web designer about how to set it up or check out various sites that offer you not only templates and techniques to generate your piece but also an opportunity to host free of charge.

RESUME KEYWORDS—A FEW MORE TIPS AND POLISHING POINTS

A keyword section may enhance your resume and tell the reader more about what you have to offer. Clustering keywords will create emphasis and trigger the attention of the computer

Areas of Expertise
CPA, State and Local Tax Sales Codes, Budgeting and Appreciation Accruals, Bonding and Tax Licensing Supervision …

Build your resume with words that identify the skills you've mastered and the responsibilities you've handled. The screening software focuses on nouns that highlight essential skills; by doing a content analysis of both print want ads and computer postings, you will glean the best and most often used and come away with the "winners" for your resume. You can try to integrate them into the body of your resume and/or you can create a special section.

Unique Skills
Team Development, Contract Negotiation, Multi-location Management, etc.

You can put this keyword section anywhere—the computer isn't fussy. Most people like it after the contact particulars and see it as a prelude to what's coming next and as an approach to networking positively using the computer.

MORE SUMMARY TIPS (SOME WORTH REPEATING)

- Use strong verbs—"implemented," "generated", "created," etc. Action verbs encourage reading.
- Use technical terms only if they enhance the description of your work. Avoid jargon—assume the reader does not know it.
- Use abbreviations cautiously and carefully.
- Use the third-person voice. Avoid "I" and refrain from using personal pronouns at all.
- Use a consistent tense and vary your sentence structure if possible.
- Avoid including any personal information about your race, marital status, religious or political affiliations, etc.

- Avoid including your references. No need for "References Available Upon Request" either.
- Avoid providing your salary expectations and history.
- Present only the truth—be honest about everything or be prepared for an immediate termination if any falsehood is discovered.
- Stick to two pages; use a third for extensive publication lists.

"Interface" and Other Buzzwords

Remember not to flower your resume with "high falutin'" words.

By trying to sound intelligent or qualified, you may end up annoying or confusing your reader. You don't want an employer to need a dictionary to discover what you really did at your last job.

Avoid buzzwords that have become cliche and words that are unnecessarily sophisticated. "Synergy," "liaise," and "grounded" are examples of buzzwords that have been overused and abused.

Say what you mean plainly and simply. For example, instead of "to interface," say "to interact." Instead of "to impact," say "to affect." Instead of "utilize," say "use."

Here's what you always should include in your resume: keywords. Recruiters use keywords to search for resumes. So choose some of the basic, important keywords in your field and pepper them throughout your resume.

Some Closing Thoughts

You have the opportunity to build a resume that will present you in the best positive light possible. It needn't be a "locked-in-cement" document. You can make changes and improvements along the way and improve the look. Your goal is to attract positive attention and to pique the curiosity of the employer to call you in for an interview.

> **ROI** (Recommendations, Opinions, and Insights)
>
> Before you press the "send" button, be sure everything you are transmitting is exactly the way you want it. No mistakes whatsoever. Retrieving a message with an incorrect first name or a T letter or a resume with a typo is nearly impossible, and the long-term error is equally difficult to repair.
>
> Be most discreet and appropriately businesslike in how you participate in any Internet job-related or networking/interactive discussion groups. This is not a back door to a dating service or an opportunity to screen for the love of your life. Stay strictly business at all times.

✳ *Summary* ✳

✳ Including all the components practiced in this book—your contact information, a Summary Profile (a good opportunity for a keywords piece, as well), Experience/Accomplishments, Education/Professional Development, and Other (Publications, Awards, Associations)—will most likely give a more complete and comprehensive picture of who you are.

✳ Using the Internet effectively can increase your exposure for interesting positions, yet spending too much time in this area will mean spending too little time getting out and meeting people who can help you.

SAMPLES

heck out these samples. You will see examples of both chronological and functional resumes for applicants who are entering the field, individual contributors, managers, and senior staff. Sample resumes for for-profit positions start on page 146. Samples for not-for-profit positions start on page 221.

ENJOY.

Health Care Resume Sample: Chronological/Entry Level

Medical Office Adminstrator
Liz Annya
1010 Canal St.
Venice, FL 46229
Phone: 803-114-7655 (Cell)
E-mail: pastagirl@hotmail.com

OBJECTIVE

To obtain an entry-level medical or health-care-related position where my problem-solving and interpersonal skills can be effectively used to contribute to the growth of the company.

EXPERIENCE/ACCOMPLISHMENTS

HOME HEALTH AIDE   03/2006 – 05/2006
Private Home Healthcare, Gatorville, Florida
• Administered medication.
• Assisted quadriplegic patient with activities of daily living.
• Changed wound dressing and provided wound care.

MORTGAGE CONSULTANT   06/2003 – 05/2004
Finagle Financial, Cashtown, Michigan
• Interviewed prospective clients and qualified borrowers.
• Evaluated and analyzed credit-worthiness with adherence to underwriting guidelines.
• Generated ten to 20 mortgage loans per month.

LOAN PROCESSOR   01/2003 – 06/2003
Mega Mortgage, Poor City, Michigan
• Analyzed credit-worthiness based on underwriting guidelines.
• Generated mortgage sales leads.
• Processed 30 to 50 loans per day.

SALES COORDINATOR   06/1995 – 07/1998
SpeedBoat Sal's, Miami, Florida
• Sold power boat training courses through phone and referrals.
• Created a marketing and advertising campaign to generate sales leads.
• Achieved a sales rate of 20 to 30 new students per week.

Health Care Resume Sample: Chronological/Entry Level, continued

PASSENGER SERVICES REPRESENTATIVE   02/1993 – 05/1995
Fly Straight Airlines Ltd., OneWayTicketVille, Florida
- Interacted with customers and located lost cargo and luggage.
- Coordinated communications between headquarters and worldwide freight offices.
- Checked cargo safety prior to loading on aircraft.

EDUCATION

05/2004 – 05/2005
Pynchum Community College, Westfield, Michigan
Pre-Nursing (3.7 GPA)

09/1999 – 06/2002
University of Bizbuzz, Rosemont, Iowa
Bachelor of Science – Business Administration with honors (Good standing).

08/1998 – 08/1999
Metropolitan College – Brooklyn, New York
General studies (3.2 GPA).

LANGUAGES/SKILLS

Mandarin, Cantonese, English, Malay, Spanish, and French (working knowledge).
Microsoft Word, Excel, Access, PowerPoint, JavaScript, HTML, Web Design.

Health Care Resume Sample: Functional/Individual Contributor

EMS Medical Assistant
Ann Phetamine
3396 Mulligan Ave., Apt. #D
Atlanta, GA 67845
(763) 429-8891
ann.med@aol.com

Objective

To obtain a position as Medical Assistant where my skills and specialized training will be effectively used to provide quality healthcare.

Background Summary

Certifications
Adult and Child BLS (CPR & AED) Certification, American Heart Association – 2005
National Registry for Certified Medical Assistant – 2005 Pending

Administrative Skills
Scheduling, MS Outlook, Medical Correspondence
Insurance Billing/Coding Bookkeeping, Computers/Typing 30 wpm
Appointment Scheduling, Mail Handling, English

Clinical Skills
Patients Charting, Medical Terminology, Electrocardiograms
Anatomy and Physiology, Blood Pressure/Vitals, Laboratory Procedures
Urine Pregnancy Test, Blood Typing, Assist in Minor Surgeries
Instrument Prep. and Autoclaving, Chemical Urinalysis, Phlebotomy, Injections
Examination Room Techniques, Tray Setup

Employment History

10/05–11/05–DR. STITCHLEY, ATHENS, GA
Medical Assistant Externship – Roomed patients, vital signs, injections, venipunctures, scheduled appointments, immigration physicals, pulling and filing charts, called in prescriptions, wrote collection letters, recorded bookkeeping charges and credits, collected fees, made collection calls.

Health Care Resume Sample: Functional/Individual Contributor, continued

2003 – HOOTENANNY HOSPITAL, TUCKERTON, GA
Certified Nurse Aide - Professionally experienced in health care settings and private duty nursing, committed to the medical profession and to quality patient care, professionalism, capability and compassion to truly integrate patient's medical and emotional care within the hospital, facility, or private duty environment, communicate well with doctors, colleagues, and patient's family, ensuring continuity of patient care

1995–2002 – MERCY SAKES REHABILITATION CENTER, RYE, NY
Certified Nurse Aide – Professionally experienced in health-care settings and private duty nursing, committed to the medical profession and to quality patient care

Education
2005 Institute for Business and Technology, Atlanta, GA
Diploma – Medical Assistant

2003 White Coat College, Birmingham, AL
Massage Therapy

2002 Can-Do Community College, Ithaca, NY
Psychology, Biology, Algebra, English, and Computers

1995 Mercy Sakes Rehabilitation Center, Rye, NY
Certified Nurse Aide Training

Health Care Resume Sample: Functional/Manager

Health Systems IT Manager

Matt Tress
43 Feather Lane
Randolphville, NJ 06689
Matt.tress@gmail.com
918-924-6650

Objective:

Project Manager (IT, Healthcare, Enterprise Application)

Professional Summary:

Dedicated professional with experience working in the health care, consumer software, and enterprise application industries. Extensive project management expertise overseeing multiple software development projects while supervising and leading cross-functional teams. Possess superb analytical and communication skills and work effectively at all organizational levels.

Summary of Achievements:

- Led multidisciplinary and technical teams in the development of highly complex web applications interfacing with internal and external systems across distributed networking environments
- Created comprehensive project plans with identification of critical paths, dependencies, and milestones while overseeing progress of project deliverables to manage scope and risk
- Expert knowledge in SDLC, software technologies, and testing methodologies
- Partnered with business subject matter experts to review requirements and develop solution alternatives
- Created quality assurance department responsible for all software development testing including the implementation of a new enterprise client/server and Web-based care management system
- Developed departmental policies, procedures, and workflow documentation to set quality and performance standards
- Responsible for testing software applications for compliance with both SOX and HIPAA regulations and reporting to internal and external auditors

Health Care Resume Sample: Functional/Manager, continued

Work Experience:

INCIDENTAL HEALTHCARE COMPANY
Supervisor Client Services 2004 – Present
Senior Business Systems Analyst
Project Manager

Education:

WESTERN MICHIGAN UNIVERSITY (B.A. – CUM LAUDE)	1996 – 1998
MAJOR: *Communications*	
MINOR: *Business Management*	
POSTGRADUATE COURSEWORK	
CCNA and CISSP certification training	2004
Intro to C++, Intro to Java, Advanced Java Programming	2000 – 2001

Languages:

HTML, SQL, CSS, Java, JSP, XML, DTD, XSD, C++, Shell Script

Systems:

XP (All Windows), AS/400, Unix (Linux, Solaris, AIX, HP-UX), OS X

Databases:

MS SQL, Oracle, Access, MySQL, DB2

Health Care Resume Sample: Functional/Senior Manager

Health Systems Senior Business Analyst

Jenn Uflect
MA, PMP
Mill Valley, CA
(415) 307-4018

OBJECTIVE

Senior Business Analyst

BACKGROUND SUMMARY

Accomplished and innovative IT professional with 21 years of successful software development on projects up to $12 million. Managed seven projects and was a principal in 25+ projects. Performed instrumental roles as business analyst, technology consultant, DBA, and programmer/analyst.

Strong background in business and technology analysis. Excel in working with primary stakeholders to understand their current problems, gathering business requirements and goals, identifying cutting-edge technology solutions, and submitting designs for management approval. Partner with management and technology professionals from concept to IT project delivery stage, and serve as a critical business and technology resource to ensure project is delivered on time, within budget, and meeting or exceeding customer specifications and business/technology objectives. Provide training and support to end-users.

Regarded as a strong communicator and peak performer who excels in creating quality management plans, ensures quality standards are met, and works diligently on IT projects to crystallize vision.

TECHNOLOGY BACKGROUND

- Complex Project Management
- Team Leadership
- IT Staff Mentoring / Coaching
- Cross-Functional Team Leadership Project Risk Analysis
- Project and Delivery Methodologies
- Change Management Leadership
- Budget Development and Planning

Health care Resume Sample: Functional/Senior Manager, continued

- Business Analysis
- Key Stakeholder Interviewing
- Requirements Gathering AND Validation
- Systems Architecture
- End-User Support
- Business Process Training
- Organizational Development
- Software Development
- Database Design and Administration Programming
- Quality Assurance
- Web Site Projects

Offer strong experience across multiple industries, including health care, pharmaceutical, education, real estate, banking, shipping, utility, insurance, retail, aerospace, and federal government.

INFORMATION TECHNOLOGY HIGHLIGHTS

Worked with Pay-Up International on an electronic bill payment application as company was eager to gain a competitive edge in this lucrative market. Project involved integrating thousands of individual bank ACH systems into the Pay-Up backbone transaction routing and payment clearing system. Project details included conducting due diligence on Pay-Up and bank information infrastructures, creating a conversion program to transmit data, overseeing technical issues related to multiple platforms, communication links, and security protocols, writing training materials, and training staff on system.

Traveled to Australia as project leader to redesign a failed Stock Status system for SuperMart Australia and ensure the viability of their $12 million investment in a national inventory management system. Introduced technology design solutions that handled over 300 million records, guaranteed a two-second user response time, and saved $3 million. Provided technical support and supervision to staff to ensure new system performed at optimal levels.

Reengineered an automated configuration management system for Heavenly Health Insurance. Technology project automatically handled hundreds of changes needed to run tests in the appropriate environment by using the right libraries and data files; as a result, high rate of errors was drastically reduced.

Managed and designed one of Force 10's most successful IT projects in years. Company provides 2,000+ eLearning products in multiple languages. This contract management system enables contracts to be stored and accessed in a database with details readily available for accountant,

Health Care Resume Sample: Functional/Senior Manager, continued

contract manager, and senior manager reports. Project details included reviewing contracts to gather requirements and design solutions, working with contract managers and attorneys to structure new contract designs, partnering with administrative staff and senior management, and defining requirements and structure of new reports. Created program and database specifications for technical staff and interacted with the business staff to resolve technical issues. Validated data entry processes and reports to resolve technical problems. Used VB and Crystal Reports with SQL Server. Designed a global order entry system in multiple languages for Force 10's global sales force and product fulfillment center in Ireland for product delivery. Project included designing a proof-of-concept for an order entry system, interviewing staff in sales, administration, and fulfillment to understand their business and technology concerns and needs, building a best-of-class infrastructure based on J2EE technology, and resolving technical and business issues.

CAREER HISTORY

BUSINESS SYSTEMS CONSULTANT – Happy Valley, CA 1985 to Present
Leveraged information technology experience to work closely with clients and focus on business analysis, process design, project management, and software development. Collaborated with 30 customers to transform their technology and business needs into practical solutions, provide the best technology solutions as a gateway for new business opportunities, accelerate reporting processes, and more. Involved in projects ranging up to $12 million and involving 40 IT professionals. Projects have focused on software development and Web site management (content, graphic design, and database integration).

SELECTED PROJECTS

Red Fence of California. In order to protect over $80 million in business processes, studied the risk to costs, reputation, agility, and ease of doing business due to the loss of the company Web site. Interviewed executives to determine business goals and how they are operationalized through the Web site. Documented the cross-functional interdependencies between the business units as they interweave with the Web site.

Cooper Construction. Challenged to secure real-time images from construction site cameras and present on-demand, time-lapsed reports to project managers. Architected program to retrieve images from cameras that had been configured as Web servers, and designed reports for customer using VB.Net.

Olson Oncology. Leveraged PhotoShop, HTML/CSS, JavaScript, ASP.NET, and Access to create kiosks for a national convention. Coordinated design and rollout efforts among graphic artists, booth projects manager, questionnaire designer, and construction professionals. Led on-site

Health Care Resume Sample: Functional/Senior Manager, continued

installation of kiosks and deployed network configuration. Kiosks were three times as successful as those in the past and generated hundreds of new sales leads.

Can-Do-IT. Designed software enhancements to track locations, maintenance, and performance of high-performance mufflers for start-up company. Gathered technology requirements by interviewing staff and understanding their needs. Project was delivered on time and within budget guidelines using Access.

Heavenly Health Insurance. Teamed with multiple stakeholders to understand and define technology system needs and design programs to comply with the National Committee for Quality Assurance. Provided technical leadership regarding system architecture and technical problem resolution. Programmed system by using VB and Crystal Reports with SQL Server.

Ramped-Up Realtors Web Site. Hired to design an automated system to retrieve information from MLS regarding new real estate properties, and transfer information and photos to a searchable, Internet database. Won approval from management on Web site design; coordinated test and deployment project components and executed project. Designed solution based on VB and Crystal Reports with SQL Server; supervised development professionals and handled technical and design issues.

REPRESENTATIVE LIST OF ADDITIONAL CLIENTS

New World Navigation… Helio Drug Stores… Dilbert's Department Stores… Mega Mortgage Securities … Southland Electric System … Hopeful Life Insurance System Group … Red Fence of Connecticut … Eveready Aircraft … Fremont Financial Services Group

TECHNICAL INVENTORY

Visual Basic.Net … ASP.Net … SQL Server … Access… Word… Excel … Visio … Project … IS … TSQL … Crystal Reports … HTML … CSS … XML … Visual Studio.net … UML/Data Modeling … OP … VBScript … J2EE … RUP … DB2 … COBOL … JavaScript… PH P… MySQL … PhotoShop … Dreamweaver … Siebel

EDUCATION/PROFESSIONAL DEVELOPMENT

Master of Arts degree, Psychology – California Institute of Integral Studies – San Francisco, CA
Bachelor of Arts degree, Economics – University of Connecticut – Storrs, CT
Certified Project Management Professional (PMP)

Banking/Finance Resume Sample: Chronological/Entry Level

Financial Analyst

Raj Mahal
Rm8888@gmail.com
(508) 808-9623

OBJECTIVE

To obtain an opportunity as a Financial Analyst that uses my quantitative and analytical skills and experience in various fields of finance.

PROFESSIONAL HISTORY

NETWORTH INDUSTRIES, HAYWARD, CA   MAR 2006 – PRESENT

Accounting Analyst

- Manage accounts payable/receivables and payroll of various for-profit and nonprofit organizations having revenues between $500K and $50M.

- Work with several corporations, banks and other financial institutions to perform financial audits for corporations and individuals.

CASH-FLOW TECHNOLOGIES LTD., HYDERABAD, INDIA   APR 2005 – SEPT 2005

Financial Analyst

- Conducted financial and risk analysis using multiple what-if scenarios for venture into the engineering services industry.

- Assisted with budgeting and project planning for plastics and packaging division.

Banking/Finance Resume Sample: Chronological/Entry Level, continued

EDUCATION

CALIFORNIA STATE UNIVERSITY, HAYWARD, CA, MAY 2006
Masters of Business Administration, Major: Finance, GPA 3.72/4.0

FINANCIAL ENGINEERING COLLEGE, NEW DELHI, INDIA, MAY 2005
Bachelor of Engineering, Major: Computer Science, GPA 3.8/4.0

Course Projects:

- Developed a comprehensive business plan to develop and market blood sugar measuring devices in rural India.

- Developed a business plan to study the feasibility of opening a personalized gift basket business in the Bay Area.

- Financial analysis of IBM and the computer industry including a detailed analysis of IBM's balance sheet between 1995 and 2004. Also provided recommendations to improve IBM's competitive position based on past performance of different divisions and market forces.

- Assessed the impact of the Financial Services Modernization Act on commercial banks.

- Analyzed the factors involved in determining risk for Employee Dishonesty Insurance.

- Designed and developed a resource planner for a hospital using a Java platform. Scheduler was used to help plan day-to-day activities such as doctor appointments and hospital bed allocation.

AREAS OF EXPERTISE

- Finance: Cash Flow Analysis, Forecasting, Budgeting, Financial Modeling, Competitive Analysis, Capital Evaluations.

- Computer: Advanced Excel, Visual Basic, VBA, Word, PowerPoint.

- ERP Related: Oracle Financials 11i, PL/SQL.

Banking/Finance Resume Sample: Chronological/Individual Contributor

---

Loans Manager

CHUCK ROAST
roast.chuck@yahoo.com
(707) 425-0778

PROFESSIONAL SUMMARY

Over ten years' experience in diverse industries, including finance, banking, retail and telecom-munications. Exceptional analytical acumen and financial competence. Self-directed with a pas-sion for quality, accuracy, and detail. Extremely tech savvy with superior abilities in process development, analytics, operations, and client services.

PROFESSIONAL EXPERIENCE

Tax Clerk, Dewey, Cheetum & Howe, Beaute, MT   **Dec 2006 – Present**
Tax reclassification research and processing of dividend income and stock distributions
Accrual portfolio accounting for estate valuations (trust, IRA, and brokerage accounts)
Quality control of trade confirmations and account statements

Accomplishments:
- Considered top performer and received increasing responsibilities
- Selected to conduct research for corporate spin-off and reorganization distributions
- Developed alternative methods resulting in increased efficiency and productivity

Teaching Asstistant, Miss Crabtree College, Andover, MA   **Aug 2005 – Aug 2006**
Taught students how to analyze problems and communicate results
Gained demand for assistance in other subjects (finance, accounting, statistics)

Project Consultant, Global Grab Inc., Spendthrift, IL   **May 1999 – Jan 2001**
Network Technician (Northpoint Communications)
Network support of Northpoint Communication's DSL Network. Trouble resolution and problem iso-lation of all WAN elements (ATM switches, DSLAMs, routers and DLCs). Opened telnet sessions and used CopperMountain software for real-time monitoring. Setup vendor meets and managed client relations. Documented testing and procedures using BOSS and Siebel databases.

Banking/Finance Resume Sample: Chronological/Individual, continued

Accomplishments:
- Used analytical and troubleshooting skills to solve network anomalies
- Coordinated multifunctional collaborations, set goals and priorities
- Created templates to improve efficiency and productivity for technicians

Logical Provisioner/LEAD, NorthComm, Lincoln Park, MI
Second-tier support, Trainer and Mentor for Logical Provisioning Testers. Supervised team of eight logical testers. Primary contact for all escalations and issues within department. Worked with ILEC Engineers for Tech Spec relations, procedures, and escalated issues.

Accomplishments:
- Selected to collaborate with Engineering for new market implementation
- Developed methods and procedures, increasing productivity 30 percent
- Enhanced leadership, interpersonal, and communication skills
- Promoted two positions higher within six months

Technical Analyst/Trainer, Intricate Internet Services, Chicago, IL
ISDN, ADSL, IDSL, and dial–up networking connectivity support to end users via oral and written communication. Handled second-tier support, mentoring and evaluation of new employees. Documentation of procedures, status, and inquiries in Vantive.

Accomplishments:
- Promoted to trainer and mentor for junior-level analysts
- Created macros to speed up documentation and increase productivity

PC Technician, Tech-Tock Systems, Indianapolis, IN   Oct 98 – May 99
Installation, maintenance and troubleshooting NT-based networks and printers as well as migrations to different locations and upgrades, which included complete teardowns/re-assembly and cable-laying. This included the setup, installation, and configuration of all network-related hardware and software, ensuring that each user had network connectivity.

Senior Proof Operator, Shield Bank, Green Brook, OH   Mar 1998 – May 1999
Encoded and endorsed checks and deposits. Verified the balance and accuracy of deposits. Maintained ranking in highest level of productivity and quality.

Banking/Finance Resume Sample: Chronological/Individual, continued

EDUCATION

Bachelor of Science in Business Administration, Corporate Finance, GPA 3.4
Lakefront State University, Chicago, IL, August 2006
Dean's List 2004, 2005, 2006

Associate in Applied Science, Computer Technology, GPA 3.73
Cubbie College, Chicago, IL, January 1999
Dean's Award, Director's Award

SKILLS AND COMPETENCIES

- Proven ability to master new software applications and technology
- Passion for continuous improvement, attention to detail, and dedication to hard work
- Effective in both team and individual settings with strong communication at all levels
- Superior ten-key, data entry and spreadsheet abilities
- Ability to manage multiple priorities under limited supervision to meet requirements

Computer Skills
- MS Office with strong knowledge of Excel and Word
- BOSS, Siebel, Vantive, Legacy, Client Central, EVP Systems, IBM On-Demand, Remedy
- Bloomberg Financial, Schwab Bond Source, Xcitek, CCH
- Win 3.1, 95/98, NT server/workstation, Sun Station
- Copperview, Openview, Harris WATT

Banking/Finance Resume Sample: Chronological/Manager

Deposits Manager

Freddie Mac
1212 Broadway
New York, NY 89945
fmac@earthlink.net
202-888-1990

OBJECTIVE

SUMMARY

- 12 years of experience managing the business and technical side of Internet B2B/B2C projects with experience in SAP, online security, and Internet technologies (e.g., HTML, CSS, RSS, XML, Perl, Java).
- Managed the development and deployment to 16 million customers of Big Budget Bank's SiteKey system, the first online banking authentication mechanism that met federal government requirements.
- Over the past ten years have deployed over 12 large-scale e-commerce/Internet projects.

EXPERIENCE/ACOMPLISHMENTS

Senior Architect   **11/2005 – 2006**
Compu Corporation – Customer Solutions Group
Worked with Fortune 50 retailers in evaluating new technologies (RFID, WIMAX, VOIP, kiosks, mobile payments, media networks, etc.) and led the design process for integrating these technologies into their business.

Project Manager (independent consultant)   **9/2005 – 11/2005**
Fast Cash Financial – Internet Service Group

Worked on creating requirements for a new authentication strategy for authentication of users signing up for new banking or loan products.

Banking/Finance Resume Sample: Chronological/Manager, continued

Project Manager (independent consultant)	**2004 – 8/2005**

Bank of Last Resort – eCommerce PMO

Managed the delivery of the SiteKey two-factor authentication project from idea to implementation in eight months that affected the login for 16 million active customers. Led the project scoping, vendor assessment, contract negotiations, design, budgets, and coordination with other business groups/vendors. Facilitated requirements sessions with technology and business teams. Regularly briefed executives (chief security officer for the bank/VP of e-commerce) on project status and customer impact issues. The project used Six Sigma DMAIC along with software development lifecycle process to create a SOA platform for Web security services that also provided for single sign-on to other vendor systems.

In 2004, managed the implementation of MS Money, consumer online funds transfer (between financial institutions) and several Web site user experience/infrastructure projects.

Independent Consultant	**2002 – 2003**

Worked on project management and technical consultant roles for technology start-ups.

Director of Alliance Services	**1999-2001**

Happy Valley Bank

Directed development of technical infrastructure and business processes needed to integrate our online offerings with those of Asian/European financial institutions. Managed all IT development and operations for the eLink division (including network security, application development, integration with vendors/partners, et al.). Built a national portal that provided business services to the 10,000 technology companies that are clients of the bank.

Project Manager	**1997 – 1999**

Likeitalot LLC - Professional Services Group

Led teams of 20+ in the implementation of e-commerce system for customers. Worked with senior management of clients (CEO/CFO/CIO/CMO) to understand their e-commerce IT/business needs and develop solutions to meet them during implementation. Worked with third-party application developers to understand their needs and lead an internal team to build a staging system, tool sets, and documentation, which decreased implementation times and costs.

IT Manager; Integrated Tech Institute; Fremont, CA	**1996 – 1997**
Senior Systems Analyst; How-to HealthCare Corp; Folsom, CA	**1995 – 1996**
Independent Consultant	**1994 – 1995**
Operations Systems Engineer; Awesome Integrators, Novato, CA	**1993 – 1994**

Banking/Finance Resume Sample: Chronological/Manager, continued

EDUCATION/PROFESSIONAL DEVELOPMENT

University: USC, Los Angeles, California
Major: Biological Sciences and Computer Science
Degree: Bachelor of Science, Date of Graduation: 8/1990

IT EXPERIENCE

Managed technical implementation of: I2's procurement system, SAP R/3, Content Management/Personalization systems (Broadvision & ATG), LDAP, VPN, Netscape & IIS Web servers, ten e-commerce systems (B2B and B2C), Oracle databases, data warehouses, OLAP tools, integration with corporate systems (CRM/HR/call centers), local area networks, wide area networks, wireless local area networks and firewalls. Used Six Sigma methodology to manage projects at Bank of Big Dreams.

Programming experience with: C, Pascal, Perl, Visual Basic, Java, JSP, HTML, XML.

Operating Systems: Solaris 2.6, Windows 95/98/NT/XP, Linux, Apple OS X

Hardware: Sun 420R, 220R, & 450, Dell, HP, and Compaq Intel based servers, HW/SW RAID and firewalls

Software: Broadvision 4.1, I2 Procurement, SAP 3.1h, Oracle 8.15, Netscape Enterprise Server 3.6, MS Internet Information Server (IIS), Apache, Verity, MS SQL server, MS Project, MS Access, Visio, MS Office Professional 7.0 (Word, Excel, PowerPoint), Adobe Photoshop, Adobe Acrobat, IQ Live, Dreamweaver

Training Courses: Software requirements analysis and design (1991), Software Verification and Validation (1992), Visual Basic Advanced Programming (1996), SAP ERP Sales and Distribution (1998), Broadvision Content Management System (1999)

Banking/Finance Resume Sample: Chronological/Senior Manager

Justin Thyme
345 Goldbrick Road
Washington, D.C.
thymeonmyside@yahoo.com
409-765-308 (cell)

OBJECTIVE:

To contribute directly as a senior financial manager to the successful future of a thriving company with a driven management team. I am a team player with strong finance, accounting, and operations experience looking to use my management, analytical, systems, finance, and accounting skills.

SUMMARY:

14+ years' finance and accounting experience. 5+ years' successfully managing staff in FP&A, G/L Accounting, and operations functions. Established and improved FP&A, accounting, and business processes, systems and controls for increased profitability estimated at 1–2% of revenue. M&A, debt and equity financing, contract negotiation, strategic planning, business planning and development, and S-1 filing experience.

EXPERIENCE/ACCOMPLISHMENTS:

SPORTS OF ALL SORTS, INC.   **Jul 06–Present**

Company is being sold. Start-up sells software and testing services for sports matching and readiness testing. Has 11 full-time employees and approximately 20 part-time employees and <$100K in revenue.

VP FINANCE AND ADMINISTRATION

- Sole contributor managing finance, accounting, HR, and administration.
- Implemented cost reductions, made Board presentations, assisted CEO in financing and company sale efforts.

PAY NOTE SYSTEMS, INC. (NASDAQ: PAYN)   **2004–Jul 06**

Sells hardware, software, and consulting services that improve online business performance and communications technologies. Generates ~$65M in sales with 265 employees worldwide.

DIRECTOR FINANCE PLANNING AND ANALYSIS

Reporting to the CFO, managed two staff in FP&A, Investor Relations, Treasury and building tenant operations functions.

- Significantly improved management reporting and FP&A processes. Team designed expense reporting database and tools, shortened annual planning process by approximately one week.
- M&A support for four acquisitions, including due diligence and revenue recognition activities.
- Negotiated reduced IR vendor costs.

Banking/Finance Resume Sample: Chronological/Senior Manager, continued

PINCHPENNY COMMUNICATIONS, INC. (NASDAQ: PPYC)   2003–2004
A $1B telecommunications company with over 4000 employees.

SENIOR FINANCE MANAGER-HOSTING DIVISION
The hosting division (formerly Geocentric, Inc.) offered company- and customer-managed data center services, shared Web site hosting, hosted software applications, and Web site management software products. Generated ~$50M in sales with 120 employees.
- Provided finance and accounting leadership to the Division. Responsible for month-end close, financial reporting, FP&A, and purchasing function.
- New product analysis, financial controls establishment, and enhancement. Significantly improved management reporting and FP&A processes.
- Supervised one purchasing assistant.
- Traveled extensively in 30 countries on five continents, 2001–2003

MONEYBELT COMMUNICATIONS, INC.   1994–2001
Nationwide wireless communications products and services provider through traditional retail and online channels. Also provided subscriber management services and software development for various Internet and wireless communications companies. Generated ~$50M in sales with 275 employees.

BUDGET DIRECTOR   *1997–2001*
- Successfully managed two staff in FP&A and two for two years in G/L accounting (month-end close, F/A, taxes, audits, and recons).
- Managed annual planning and rolling forecasts, financial reporting, financial analysis and modeling, cash flow projections.
- Directed and performed analysis related to cash flow, profit planning, capital expenditures, M&A, competitor and industry analyses and new business ventures.
- Facilitated proper implementation and control of budgeted plans. Ensured proper business partnership with various functional areas.
- Final approval authority for product pricing.
- Significantly shortened close cycle. Established accounting procedures and controls and implemented system for billing and reporting sales taxes nationwide.
- Managed implementation of Windows-based accounting, inventory, and distribution system. Process leader in launch of company's online start-up MoneyTalks.com. Designed sales, customer service, site content maintenance, and accounting processes.
- Managed product planning and distribution functions (one year) along with FP&A and G/L accounting.
- Approved inventory purchases, negotiated sales of excess inventory, established planning process for new product lines, enhanced systems and procedures.
- Indirectly managed up to 20 distribution employees.

Banking/Finance Resume Sample: Chronological/Senior Manager, continued

SENIOR FINANCIAL ANALYST   *1994–1997*
- Responsible for FP&A and financial reporting.
- Projects in M&A, opening and closure of a major facility, attempted IPO, senior debt restructuring, and equity rounds.
- Determined NPV, IRR of new business and created financial models. Company realized significant savings from efforts.
- Coordinated portions of the month-end close.
- Responsible for Board presentations and maintaining the company's banking relationship.

GASGUZZLER USA PRODUCTION COMPANY, INC.   **1988–1994**
A major domestic oil and gas producer.

ACCOUNTING ANALYST   *1993–1994*
- Created models, developed accounting procedures, analysis, and reports for management.
- Recognized opportunity to alter accounting policy to reclassify certain assets. Resulted in over $300K savings to company.

ANALYST   *1991–1993*
- Created models and analysis to reduce royalty burden.
- $2.5M cash savings in 1992–1993.

ACCOUNTANT   *1988–1991*
- Calculated and made royalty payments to federal government.
- Reconciled G/L accounts. Performed monthly variance analysis of royalty payments. Responded to internal and external audit inquiries.

EDUCATION/PROFESSIONAL DEVEOPMENT:
- Piggy Bank University, Boston, MA, MBA Finance and Information Systems concentrations, March 2001.
- Cookie Jar College, Philadelphia, PA, additional accounting and finance course work.
- University of Hard Knocks, Wheeling, VA, BA Business Economics (Finance Concentration), March 1989.
- Part-time marketing consulting work at SCU for Jamcracker, Inc. a start-up application service provider.

SKILLS:
Programming language: SQL
Computer programs: Excel with macros, Access, Solomon/Microsoft Dynamics, MS Enterprise Reporting, Oracle, SAS, Business Objects, Macola, Hyperion, Word, Powerpoint, Crystal, TM1, FRx, QuickBooks

Operations Resume Sample: Chronological/Entry Level

OPERATIONS ASSISTANT

R. U. LISSENING
657 Mustang Way, Hooperville, OK 98734
(789) 245-9083, robert.lessening@earthlink.net

OBJECTIVE
To bring my abilities and Operations Management skills to your organization.

SUMMARY PROFILE
Proficient in start-up design, management and implementation. Professional in appearance, speaking, and writing. Ability to relate and communicate ideas and goals to all individuals within an organization.

Skills and Abilities:
Excellent team player
Payroll, AR and AP management
Effective training development and facilitator
Comprehensive human resource management
Total facilities and preventative maintenance management
Property and leasing management
Proficient information systems management

EMPLOYMENT EXPERIENCE
CARLSON AND ASSOCIATES, TULSA, OK   Nov 2005 – Aug 2006
Operations Management Trainee
Provided health care consulting services for Senior Living Communities. Assessed, designed and implemented regulatory, financial, and operational programs to attain optimum performance for the client. Includes financial, marketing, facilities maintenance, human resource developmented were training. All programs are customized and produced to client's needs and specifications. Responsibilities included total healthcare operations management. Every aspect of the facilities' management was supervised, including budget development/implementation, regulatory assessment/enforcement, marketing analysis/management, and human resource recruitment/training and supervision.

EDUCATION/PROFESSIONAL DEVELOPMENT
UNIVERSITY OF OKLAHOMA
Bachelor of Science, Operations Management   June 2005

Operations Resume Sample: Chronological/Individual Contributor

Certified Internet Webmaster   Aug 2005
HVAC Technician Program/ EPA Certification   July 2005

MEDICAL BILLING OPERATIONS MANAGER

Shelia Just
1455 Piedmont Ave
McLean, VA 23325
(757) 784-4322

OBJECTIVE

To obtain a project manager or operations manager role in a major hospital or medical center billing administration department

WORK HISTORY

NATIONAL HEALTHCARE MANAGEMENT (NHM)   02/04 – 02/07

Billing Director
NHM is a physician-owned medical billing company for Medical Center Radiologists (seven locations, 45 physicians) and Pathology Sciences Medical Group (five locations, ~20 physicians) with combined annual revenues of over $31 million. I was responsible for all NHM operations and employed 57 personnel that were under my direction. Major responsibilities included:

- Monitored and analyzed accounts receivable and monthly/yearly revenues
- Critiqued staffing needs, approved new hires, and proposed annual pay increases (final approval to be given by Executive Director and BOD)
- Reporting of weekly, monthly and yearly billing financials to Medical Center Radiologists and Pathology Sciences Medical Group for BOD and shareholders meetings
- Employee and Patient Relations – assisted with resolution of escalated matters
- Negotiated insurance contracts for Medical Center Radiologists and Pathology Sciences Medical Group; monitored insurance contracts for compliance with terms and payment of negotiated allowed amounts
- Facilitated coding and billing audits by outside consultants every 18 months
- Prepared and revised NHM Guidelines and Procedures for Billing and Contract Manual; frequently reviewed procedures and implemented changes for process improvement (efficiency, quality, etc.)

Operations Resume Sample: Chronological/Individual Contributor, continued

- Prepared and revised job descriptions, salary bands, and performance evaluation forms

EDUCATION/PROFESSIONAL DEVELOPMENT

Radford University, Peroria, IL, May 2004
Cum Laude, BA, Medical Administration

CURRENT CERTIFICATIONS

Radiology Coding Certified by RCCB
Emergency Medical Technician Certified
Certified in Search and Rescue

COMPUTER SKILLS/SOFTWARE EXPERIENCE

IDX/Groupcast Medical Billing System
CPU Medical Billing System
Proficient in Word & Excel
Cognos Reporting system – Analyzer

PROFESSIONAL SOCIETY MEMBERSHIPS

Radiology Business Management Association
Professional Coders of Tidewater, local chapter of American Academy of Professional Coders
Hampton Roads Medical Group Management Association
Virginia Chapter, American Association of Healthcare Administrative Management

Operations Resume Sample: Chronological/Manager

OPERATIONS MANAGER

Z. DePlane
Seattle, WA 23769
(345) 456-768
plane.z@yahoo.com

OBJECTIVE

Obtain an Operations Manager role with a high-growth company using top-rated testing, programming, or database work.

SUMMARY OF QUALIFICATIONS

Managing the designing and building of multi-tier Visual Basic projects
Managing the designing and building of Access databases
Programming and administering SQL databases
Managing the designing and building of a Web site using ASP and HTML
Manually testing programming, database, and Web projects

WORK EXPERIENCE

CompassPoint Corporation, Seattle, WA	**May 2006 – September 2006**
Document Manager, processor, electronic assembler and tester	
Lighthouse Technologies, Seattle, WA	**September 2003 – January 2006**
Imaging/Reprographics Manager	
Simac Software Services, Kent, WA	**February 2001 – August 2003**
Software Development Manager	
Vosberg Corporation, Woodinville, WA	**October 1994 – May 2000**
Electronics Operations Manager	
Samoyed Corporation, Bethell, WA	**April 1993 – March 1994**
Electronic Technician	

Operations Resume Sample: Chronological/Manager, continued

EDUCATION /PROFESSIONAL DEVELOPMENT

Widmere College, Bellevue, WA, December 1992
BS Degree in IT/Programming

Oroton Vocational Technical Institute, Redhill, WA, June 1988
Completed a two-year Certificate in Electronics.

SOFTWARE BACKGROUND

Visual Basic, Access, Excel, ASP, HTML, MS SQL Server Administration, MS SQL Server Programming, Technical Writing, System Analysis

HARDWARE BACKGROUND

Tested, troubleshot, and repaired computers, printers, monitors, AM/FM receivers, tape recorders, car audio, pulse oximeters, custom-designed control and monitoring equipment.

Procedure:

- Tested all controls, functions, inputs, outputs.

- Determined cause of any problem found.

- Corrected cause of problem.

- Retested unit to confirm problem had been corrected.

- Retested all other controls, functions, inputs, outputs to check for any new problems created by repair process.

- Documented work done on unit.

Operations Resume Sample: Chronological/Manager, continued

ADDITIONAL COURSEWORK

Client Programming I (Visual Basic)
Develops applications for client computers in a client/server environment. Students learn data validation, debugging and error handling, file manipulation, and developing Active X Code Components.

Database Administration
Develops the concepts and skills required to perform the duties of Database Administrator (DBA) in organizations using large relational databases. Students develop coherent plans for security, disaster recovery, backup and restore, replication, and other administrative functions, including the creation and use of SQL scripts to automate administrative tasks.

Database Applications
Develops beginning through advanced database skills using Microsoft Access on the personal computer.

SQL Server: Server Programming
Introduces server programming in a client/server environment. Students learn to create, manipulate, and troubleshoot databases, tables, and views; ensure data integrity with defaults, rules, and triggers; and develop stored procedures and security.

Systems Analysis
Examines the system-development cycle in depth. Topics include problem identification, problem solving, and information-gathering techniques. Current structured tools are used to describe business rules and objects, data flow, data structures, and process flow and documentation. Creative problem solving and working in a team environment are stressed.

Web Database Development
A project-oriented, team-based exercise in developing a database-centric corporate intranet site. Students use a number of tools including Visual Basic, Visual Basic Script, and Visual InterDev. Major emphasis on student-focused learning of new applications.

Operations Resume Sample: Chronological/Senior Manager

OPERATIONS AND PRODUCTION DIRECTOR

I.M. Sirius
101 Swan Way
Miami, FL 33111
siriuswork@gmail.com
967-0440-1168

Summary Profile

Employed as an Incident and Problem Manager for Toyota Corporation. Built a skill base ranging from IT Manager for a 4000+ user base, to Human Resource Manager for a small organization, to development and deployment of a major project migration.

A committed and integral employee with professional accomplishments and established relationships.

Current and prior positions have included the following job functions and more:

- Project Management
- Operations Management
- Test Plan Development
- Information Analyst
- Human Resource Manager/Recruiter
- Forecasting/Budget Planning
- Network Migration
- Metric Evaluation
- Contract Negotiation
- Crisis Management Documentation
- Training Instructor
- Incident and Problem Management

Operations Resume Sample: Chronological/Senior Manager, continued

Chronology of Experience

COMPUWARE CORPORATION   August 2003 to present

Industry: Automotive, Miami, FL
Position: Incident and Problem Manager (technical and nontechnical)
Environment: MS Workspace, Multi Tier DB, North America Infrastructure Scope
Tools: Lotus Notes, MS Access, MS Excel, Mainframe

Overview:

Promoted to Incident and Problem Manager for North America IT Organization. Defuse IT-related problems for all North America sectors (i.e., Powertrain, Manufacturing, Develop Product). Create and evaluate corrective action plans for all performing suppliers. Develop and maintain metrics in order to stay in tune with the vendor performance and process stability. Manage Service Desk, Availability, Change and Patch Projects exercising ITIL framework. Served as Site Manager for client base of 4000+ hardware/software/mainframe users. Ranked as high -evel Project Manager reporting directly to Management Council. Created high-level standards for infrastructure support. Supported and deployed North America operating system migration. Created Crisis Recovery Process/Document to support business and technical operations in the event of a catastrophe. Participated in many projects in which I exercised the Standard SDP 21 process methodologies throughout each stage of the project life cycles. Served as liaison to third-party vendors in effort to manage contract requirements.

CONTRACT PROFESSIONALS INC.   March 1998 to April 2003

Industry: Automotive, Birmingham, AL
Position: Project Manager/Buyer/Contract Negotiator
Environment: MS Windows 95/98/NT, LAN/WAN, UNIX
Tools: Lotus Notes, MS Access, MS Excel, MS Word, MS Project, MS PowerPoint, MS Netmeeting, Mainframe

Overview:

Purchased and tested product development components for engineering/design community. Compared cost metrics. Wrote and launched process modules for business improvement. Conducted billing review of third-party vendor, resulting in major cost savings. Participated in special projects exercising SDP 21 structure. Negotiated contract interests at local levels. Created position requisitions according to project requirements. Reviewed all resumes received by consulting firms. Wrote practices and procedures according to project scope. Conducted new employee orientation. Developed and distributed project news publication. Created and explained resource cost metrics to management board. Increased service level performance from consulting vendors. Balanced project budget.

Operations Resume Sample: Chronological/Senior Manager, continued

Fortune Finder Bank Headquarters   October 1997 to February 1998

Industry: Financial, Houston, TX
Position: Training Instructor
Environment: LAN/WAN
Tools: Mainframe, online application system specific to environment, MS Publisher, MS Power-Point, MS Word, MS Excel

Overview:

Instructed a class on mortgage-based software products. Wrote training manuals customized to core teaching techniques. Rated employee skill levels according to test factors. Traveled to national branches to resolve product issues.

SUPERIOR DATA SYSTEMS   October 1995 to November 1997

Industry: Business Services – Corporate Staff, Austin, TX
Position: Employee Business Training and Retirement Specialist
Environment: Mainframe, LAN/WAN
Tools: MS Access, MS Excel, MS Word, MS PowerPoint

Overview:

Prepared and conducted behavioral interviewing process for prospective new hires. Trained new-employee class modules. Promoted to Subject Matter Expert. Conducted calculation drafts for pension benefit program. Performed orientation for eligible retiree candidates. Consulted with major medical, insurance, and other investment firms to provide financial specifics to retiree candidates. Solved inconsistent process methods according to legal guidelines. Presented written statements to legal department for fraud review. Evaluated warranty expirations upon receipt of customer concerns. Disputed claims from customers and legal representatives.

Additional experience from 1993 to 1995 not listed in this resume. Information available upon request.

Education/Professional Development

Bachelor of Science – Business Studies
University of Phoenix

Associate Degree – Business Studies
Macomb Community College

PMI Registered
ITIL Certified

Operations Resume Sample: Chronological/Senior Manager, continued

Software/Hardware/Tools Skills Summary

Microsoft Access, Telnet Router/Remote Access
Microsoft Word, Disaster Recovery DB_2, Internet Explorer
Microsoft PowerPoint, Lotus Notes, Microsoft Excel
Microsoft Netmeeting, Microsoft Project, Microsoft Windows
(95/98/2000)
Compaq Hardware
Hewlett-Packard

Ancillary Skills

Ethernet Tivoli
VPN WinInstall
Switches Adobe
QuarkXpress
MS Publisher

Sales and Marketing Resume Sample: Chronological/Entry Level

SALES ASSOCIATE, ONLINE MARKETING

Kenny Celle
56 Fostoria Way
Martinez, CA 45892
714-0909-5623
k.celle@hotmail.com

OBJECTIVE:

Seeking Business / Sales Professional role supporting a company with a Web site or digital presence demonstrating track record of exceeding sales quotas and revenue growth expectations.

SUMMARY OF QUALIFICATIONS:

- Motivated sales professional
- Able to explain complex ideas and systems to potential clients in a clear and concise manner
- Superior presentation and communication skills
- Growing expertise in contract negotiations
- Ability to create and maintain excellent client relationships
- Self-starter, excellent in multi-tasking
- Able to quickly absorb and disseminate new information
- Extremely organized, personable, well liked by co-workers

PROFESSIONAL EXPERIENCE:

Smartsave.com LLC, Fernando Valley, CA   **July 2005 – Present**
Sales Associate
Quicksave.com is a profitable Internet marketing company.
- Mastered and successfully implemented marketing and sales programs to attract and retain retail clients.
- Consulted with retail corporations with regards to profitable online marketing strategies.
- Created and customized marketing plans based on the specific needs of individual companies.
- Established retail client accounts that make up 90% of company revenue.

Sales and Marketing Resume Sample: Chronological/Entry Level, continued

Pronto Television, Inc., Chico, CA   **January – June 2005**
Sales Intern
Pronto TV is a microwave TV company.
* Assisted in promotion of all channels in the Bakersfield, CA market through long-term leases or outright sales.
* Helped negotiate lease agreements for channel rights.
* Competed successfully in FCC auctions with prevailing high bid in market.

EDUCATION/PROFESSIONAL DEVELOPMENT:

University of Northern Florida, Jacksonville, FL
BSBA in Management, May 2004

Certifications and Recognitions:
* Handlers' License for Internet Vendor Applications, January 2006
* VOLP trade organization Certification for Sales and Marketing of Microwave Digital Media, April 2005
* Dean's Award for Internet Business Administration Program, March 2003

Sales Resume Sample: Functional/Individual Contributor

SALES MANAGER, FASHION INDUSTRY

Dee Ziner
855 Fifth Avenue # 220, New York, NY 19087
718-824-5444, Ziner.d@gmail.com

SUMMARY PROFILE

Experienced sales and marketing professional and business management. Proven ability to rapidly gain expertise in new product lines or services and frequently recognized for outstanding proficiency. Proven ability to negotiate purchase product contracts, develop alternate sources of procurement, and manage accounts. Proven record of reducing cost and providing long- and short-term valuable planning.

PROFESSIONAL EXPERIENCE

Fashion First Agency, New York, NY   **2004 – Present**

Sales Manager
- Develop sales and marketing strategic plan to generate new client base within fashion industry.
- Deploy cold-calling and telemarketing techniques to identify key prospects.
- Develop client objective-assessments and enhance our initial communication method to deliver high-impact sales presentation.
- Generate new clients; conduct on-site presentations for multi-level executives within large corporations.
- Lead and manage marketing strategies across two business units and 10 brands.
- Manage marketing positioning efforts and lead brand-development initiatives that differentiate company's services; ensure compelling value propositions and create detailed market plans and new business opportunities.
- Increase sales 25% in eight months.

Isle of Last Resort, Melbourne, FL   **1997 – 2004**

Sales and Marketing Liaison Manager
- Effectively established communication system between sales directors and marketing director, which saved the company $700,000.
- Implemented channel of exchange for regional sales manager and marketing executive with national gross of $600 million a year.

Sales Resume Sample: Functional/Individual Contributor, continued

- Met and exceeded sales and marketing quota in the each year.
- Developed marketing and sales incentive strategy for sub-contractors that increased profit and productivity.
- Assumed significant role in piloting integration of new technologies within the company.
- Developed customer relation strategy and rapid problem-solving method.

EDUCATION/PROFESSIONAL DEVELOPMENT

Williams College, Orchard Park, FL
Business / Marketing, BA, 1997

Sales Resume Sample: Chronological/Manager

Sales & Finance Manager

Shirley Imacloser
300 North Beale St.
Las Vegas, NV 89183
672-109-452
salesgirl711@yahoo.com

SUMMARY:

Strong passion for sales and love of the close. Assertive, not afraid to take chances and live on the edge of spontaneity. Exceptional skills in networking with clients and building strong relations. Honest, dependable. efficient, hard working, able to think on feet , develop independent ideas and work well with appreciative, respectful people. A fast learner, detail oriented, with superb communication skills.

EXPERIENCE:

RideFast Motorsports, Montague, Florida   **4/2004 – Present**
Sales/Finance Manager Executive
Experienced in finance, sales, and GM duties. Ran a sales department successfully, selling at a 100K and more a month. Supervised the finance department and was acting GM for three months when GM left the organization. Gained many valuable connections in theimporrs industry and have a large customer relations base.

Bentley Rolls-Royce, Las Vegas, Nevada   **11/2003 – 3/2004**
Sales Manager Executive
This is a high-line dealership. Sold new Bentleys and Rolls-Royces and became very familiar with an extensive variety of used high-line and exotic cars such as Land Rover, Mercedes, BMW, Ferrari, and Lamborghini. There was a need to create a loyal client base as well as an impressive amount of daily follow-up with prospective clients given by leads.

Honda, Las Vegas, Nevada   **10/2001 – 11/2003**
Sales Manager Executive
Honda/Kawasaki of Las Vegas is a prominent motorsports group. It is an extremely large company with over 30 stores nationwide. In sales for almost a year; excelled and was promoted to floor manager and closer.

Sales Resume Sample: Chronological/Manager, continued

Farmers Insurance, Las Vegas, Nevada   8/2000 – 8/2001
Insurance Sales Producer
Specialized in selling motorcycle insurance and worked closely with motorsport dealerships. Enjoyed turning in work that regularly exceeded sales revenue generation goals.

EDUCATION/PROFESSIONAL DEVELOPMENT:

University of Minnesota
Duluth, Minnesota
B.A., 4/2000

Kalamath College
Brainerd, Minnesota
A.A., 5/1996

AFFILIATIONS:

10/1998 – 10/2000 Sales Internship, BMW, certificate of successful luxury sales training

1/2000 – 3/2000 GM Automobile Marketing 2.0 program for advanced salesmanship; winner of GM trainee new sales strategy award

6/1999 – 9/1999 GM customer service training; top 2% in class

Sales Resume Sample: Functional/Senior Manager

SENIOR SALES MANAGER, START-UP

Ken U. Believeit
901 Weegman Street
Oakland, CA 89702
510-826-3312
amazingsales@yahoo.com

Objective

To use my extensive senior management skills by working for a start-up company or a company with a new product or service that needs to fill its sales funnel.

Qualifications

- 20+ years' professional sales management experience, including business-to-business, telecommunications, and developing marketing and sales programs to dominate markets.
- Excellent at development and execution of strategic sales plans and account management programs.
- Successful in managing sales channels.
- Strong customer advocate with creative, dependable, and reliable problem-solving skills.
- Lead by example and work well with others.
- Excellent written and verbal skills.
- Strong problem-solving skills with a focus on customer value and relationship development.
- Proven track record of meeting/exceeding sales quotas/goals.

Experience

Venue Vision, Oakland, CA   **2005 – 2007**
Lead Generation Manager

- Generated leads for Web-based quality management software used for ISO9000, AS9100, ISO13485, ISO27000, and ITIL certification.
- Set up local seminars and online demonstrations.
- Accomplished data miner and data prospector.
- Call to CEOs, CFOs, CIOs, Security Directors, Regulatory Affairs Managers, and Quality Control Managers of major corporations throughout the U.S.

Sales Resume Sample: Functional/Senior Manager, continued

Larson's Leads, San Francisco, CA   **2004 – 2005**
Lead Generation Specialist

- Generated service and sales leads for warehouse equipment.
- Updated and added to current database through cold calling.
- Initiated an average of 50 cold calls per hour.

Pepco, San Ramon, CA   **1997 – 2004**
Customer Service/Inside Sales Manager

- Tasked with developing new install base and new channel partners for this inside sales position.
- Focused on vertical customer acquisition strategies and programs.
- Set executive-level one-on-one teleconferences and appointments.
- Lead generation through cold calling and other prospecting methods.
- Conducted surveys for after-sales reports.

Unitech, Pleasant Valley, CA   **1988 – 1997**
Customer Service/Inside Sales, Asstistant Manager

- Provided telephone customer support.
- Acquired and developed new customer and account relationships that added value to the business.
- Generated leads through prospecting and cold calling, both in-person and via telephone.
- Developed and executed marketing and sales programs that produced new business and also allowed the company to dominate the business in Southern California.
- Received two promotions from upper management for my performance.

ROI International, Ventura, CA   **1985 – 1988**
Sales Account Representative

- Telephone sales of business products.
- Experienced using a variety of sourcing techniques, including cold calling.
- Serviced and supported current clients while generating additional new business.
- Sold and managed accounts throughout Southern California.

Sales Resume Sample: Functional/Senior Manager, continued

Education/Professional Development

Loyola Marymount College
Brewster, NY
MA, Economics, magna cum laude, May 1985

City College of New York
New Paultz, NY
BA, Business Administration, cum laude, June 1983

Technical Skills:

Experienced in using Sugar, ACT, TMS, TouchStar, Salesforce.com, Digisoft, and other calling and CRM programs.

Human Resources Resume Sample: Chronological/Entry Level

JUNIOR RECRUITER

H.R. READY
(810) 462-2878
1980 Asheville Rd.
Arlington, PA 19001
ready.h.r@yahoo.com

OBJECTIVE:

Seeking a Human Resources Recruiter position within a fun, fast-paced environment

SUMMARY:

- Independent, self-motivated, work well under pressure, goal-oriented
- Consistent, reliable, and persistent
- Mastered excellence in group settings
- Strong communication skills demonstrated by the presentation of numerous projects
- Proficient in Microsoft Word, Microsoft Excel, Microsoft Outlook, Microsoft PowerPoint, PC Recruiter, and Internet

WORK EXPERIENCE:

Robyn & Merion Inc.   **12/2005 – Present**
Assistant Recruiter
- Source, screen, and evaluate potential candidates
- Maintain a recruiting load of five to 12 openings
- Coordinate, moderate, and direct the selection and evaluation process with hiring managers and decision makers
- Conduct and evaluate reference and verification checks
- Represent the company at job fairs and other recruiting events
- Placed into the company's manager program for exceeding my recruiting goals

Human Resources Resume Sample: Chronological/Entry Level, continued

H.R. International	10/2005 – 12/2005

Intern/Associate Staffing Consultant

* Created client job specs and candidate progress reports
* Cold calling for potential candidates
* Researched using PC Recruiter

Outsourcing Services Inc.	6/2005 – 8/2005

* Called Center Representative for DirecTV
* Called customers to receive overdue payments
* Answered customer service-related questions
* Used internal computer system

EDUCATION:

University of Arkansas
B.S., General Management, August 2005
Concentrations in Marketing and Human Resources

Selected Courses:
* Advertising and Sales Promotion
* Human Resource Staffing
* Fundamentals of Business Communication
* Human Resource Management
* Retail Management
* Compensation and Performance Management
* Market Research

Human Resources Resume Sample: Chronological/Individual Contributor

HUMAN RESOURCES COACH AND TRAINER

Wendy Daye
356-B Fairfax Ave., Reston, VA 87656
390-655-378, w.daye@yahoo.com

Profile:

Proven HR professional, outstanding communicator, coach, and trainer with uncompromising integrity and an inherent drive to succeed looking for a growth-oriented HR staffing business with proven track record of expansion and success.

Work History:

Creative Touch Interiors, Reston, VA   **Oct 2004 – present**
Senior HR Specialist
- Promoted and tasked with ownership of leading and mentoring three field offices, including staffing, communications, leadership partnering, associate relations, training, and workers' compensation.
- Direct report of HR Coordinator, development of three cross-functioning Office Managers new to HR responsibilities.
- Lead Associate Roundtable and Safety Team effecting positive change and increased morale across our organization.
- Established recruitment relationships with local high schools, tech schools, and universities, including Student Days, Career Fairs, and successful Internship program currently in consideration nation-wide.
- Successful placement of crucial positions, including Production Manager, Safety Manager, and Design Center Manager.

HirePros, Inc.   **Feb 2003 – Sept 2004**
Human Resources Specialist
- Instrumental in the roll-out of post-acquisition companywide training covering attendance, respect, and OSHA compliance training; includes management training and associate open forums.
- Created training materials, train-the-trainer sessions and conducted training on FISH!, harassment, performance development, teambuilding, effective communication, conflict resolution, P&L's for the nonfinancial manager, and succession planning.

Human Resources Resume Sample: Chronological/Individual, continued

- Named "Master Trainer" on Leadership Skills, Conflict Resolution, and Performance Management.
- Investigations of EEOC and workers' compensation cases as well as sensitive associate code of conduct issues.
- Strategic partner to management with regard to performance management, training initiatives, and employee relations.
- Created and delivered interview skills training for management, reducing turnover by 11%.
- Responsible for recruiting all non-exempt positions.

Landing Zone Systems, Inc., Reston, VA   **Jan 2001 – Feb 2002**
Human Resources Consultant
- Researched, evaluated, negotiated, implemented, and administered company-wide benefits programs, including health care, dental, short- and long-term disability, and life insurance.
- Developed and implemented training on diversity and maintaining international relationships.
- Researched, developed, wrote, and edited the Employee Policies Handbook, thereby lowering the director liability insurance premium.
- Handled the North American office closure, including all benefit issues, severance packages, etc.
- Recruited for all technical and leadership-level positions.

LightSpeed Access Corp., Herndon, VA   **Jan 2000 – Jan 2001**
Human Resources Generalist
- Involved in all aspects of the Human Resources Department, including benefits administration, payroll, EEOC investigations, training development, and employee relations.
- Created and conducted corporate management training on coaching and counseling.
- Researched, evaluated, and implemented companywide fair employment practices training for 550 employees across multiple corporate divisions and locations.
- Researched, evaluated, and developed cost analysis reports on corporate staffing options, which influenced the company's recruiting strategy-saving over 25k annually in placement fees and agency retainers.
- Wrote, edited, and communicated Human Resources corporate policies and procedures across multiple corporate divisions and locations.
- Helped create company wide annual review policies, tracking procedures, and management-friendly forms.

Human Resources Resume Sample: Chronological/Individual, continued

Education:–

Lyconium University – Charlottesville, VA
Bachelor's in Liberal Arts: Psychology and Human Development, May 1999

Training and Certifications:

Other courses include:
- PHR / HRIC Certification
- Risk Management – WATCH! certified
- Certified FISH! Philosophy Implementation trainer
- Certified Self Representation (Union Awareness) trainer
- Certified Kenexa 360 coach

Software Skills:

Proficient with Microsoft Windows operating systems and many software applications, including:
- Operating Systems: Microsoft Windows 3.1, Windows 95, Windows 98, Windows NT, Office 2000, Office ME, Mac OS.
- Word Processing: Microsoft Word 97, Word 98, Word 2000.
- Presentations Software: Microsoft PowerPoint, Visio.
- Spreadsheet Software: Microsoft Excel.
- Accounting Software: Quickbooks, Clients and Profits.
- Payroll Software: ADP / Reportsmith, Paychex / Report Writer.
- Recruiting Software: PeopleClick

Human Resources Resume Sample: Functional/Manager

HUMAN RESOURCES RECRUITMENT MANAGER

Sandy Beech
1433 NE 118th, Jacksonville, FL 33843
s.beech@yahoo.com, 678-933-0444

Objective:

Seeking a professional human resource management position using proven skills in recruiting, staffing, training, organizational development, and management with the expressed desire to improve organizational performance and increase customer satisfaction.

Career Highlights:

Recruiting/Staffing
- Over 20 years of diverse and challenging recruiting/staffing experience with increasing levels of responsibility, consistently turning low-yielding zones into top performers
- Recognized expert in behavioral interviewing, effectively screening and matching personal desires to the needs of the organization
- Selected as recruiting manager well ahead of peers, producing winning team first year assigned, doubling previous management production

Training and Education Management
- Developed and instructed numerous training modules
- Managed the total recruiting education and training process for a recruiting force of over 550 recruiters and managers in 17 Western States
- Developed training policies and procedures for a national organization
- Designed training program for new recruiters, which resulted in improved quality of life and performance
- Developed and instructed management training covering training, accountability, counseling techniques, discipline without punishment, and general leadership and management concepts

Leadership and Management
- Natural team builder and leader
- Supervised and managed a large-scale recruiting force in Dallas, Texas
- Executed a complete turn around in production and attitude in less than one year
- Produced the most new hires in the organization's history
- Analyzed sales trends, devised procedural changes or training programs to address deficient areas, and executed and monitored actions

Human Resources Resume Sample: Functional/Manager, continued

Planning, Coordinating, and Organizing
- Managed a number of individual long-term projects involving hundreds of others, including the reorganization of recruiting zones and districts in a 16-state region
- Expert planner, able to effectively handle multiple tasks in a high-intensity, time-sensitive environment
- Coached recruiters and recruiting managers on time management, prioritization, and planning techniques
- Developed exceptional span of control techniques, enhancing productivity despite extreme geographical separation

Human Resources Generalist
- Negotiated salaries
- Explained benefits
- Established legal employment documentation
- Key member of the succession planning committee

Communication Skills
- Polished speaker and writer with strong conceptual skills
- Developed and delivered numerous presentations to applicants, community leaders, and educators
- Instructed hundreds of hours of class time annually, instructing managers and executives on sales, recruiting, marketing, training, and leadership and management issues
- Wrote effective and persuasive communications for the CEO
- Persuaded radio and television

Technology Skills
- Microsoft Outlook, Word, Excel, PowerPoint, Internet Explorer
- Expert on Internet use and capabilities
- Resumix
- Act 7.0

Work History:

Lockstep Staffing, Recruiter, Fort Scott, KS	**July 2002 to Dec 2006**
CareerStaff Unlimited, District Manager, Hope, VA	**July 2001 to July 2002**
StaffRite Solutions, Recruiting Manager, Newark, DE	**Aug 2000 to July 2001**
Team Business Solutions, Tech Recruiter, Rodan, DE	**Aug 1999 to Aug 2000**
Air Force Recruiting, HR Manager, Randolph AFB, TX	**Jan 1995 to Aug 1999**

Education:

Master of Business Administration, St. Luke's University, Dallas, TX, August, 1999

Baccalaureate of Science, Business Management, Texarkana University, Houston, TX, December 1995

Human Resources Resume Sample: Functional/Senior Manager

RECRUITMENT PROJECT MANAGER

Belle Ringer
667 Liberty Street
Philadelphia, PA 19127
267-560-5007
belle.r@humancapital.com

SUMMARY:

Senior professional Contract and Project Recruiter, Recruitment Project Manager, and Recruitment Process Strategist with a track record of successfully completing consulting engagements in a variety of industries for clients nationwide. Broad knowledge of HR practices and employment law. You will find that I am motivated by success and a natural leader. I am seeking a consulting role where my experience, motivation, leadership skills, and creativity will help my client exceed business goals.

CONSULTING ENGAGEMENT OVERVIEW: **1998–2007**

Consultant to Comcast Communications, Philadelphia, Pennsylvania, to support Comcast's National Customer Service Senior Leadership team. Positions included Vice President of Process Optimization, Director of Customer Service Development, Director of Customer Retention Operations, Manager of Customer Service Operations, Manager of Technical Operations Planning and Analysis, Senior Director of Technical Services, Senior Director of Fulfillment, Senior Director of Contractor Management, and other senior management roles. Comcast is the largest provider of cable services in the U.S. and one of the world's leading communications companies.

Consultant to UltraMail Communications, Pittsfield, Massachusetts, to manage UltraMail's outsourced recruitment function, including developing processes, strategies, and uncovering recruiting sources. Candidates included Director of Marketing, Director of Software Engineering, Business Analyst, Software QA, Database Developer, ASP.NET Developer, and C# .NET Developer. UltraMail Communications is an industry-leading telecommunications solutions firm.

Consultant to Omniverse, Sparta, New Jersey, as Project Manager for a large outsourced staffing function. Responsible for review and execution of recruitment strategies and processes. Candi-

Human Resources Resume Sample: Functional/Senior Manager, continued

dates included Product and Project Management, Client Management, Operational Management, Business Development, Software Development, Technical Support, Engineering, and QA in the United States and internationally. Omniverse is a world leader in prepaid telecom billing solutions.

Consultant to CNET Networks, Stirling, New Jersey and Chelmsford, Massachusetts, to recruit technology candidates for both markets. Candidates included Software Engineers and Network Operations Engineers. CNET Networks is a leading provider of interactive content.

Consultant to Hammaker Car Rental Group to source candidates for operational and management positions in the northeastern and southeastern United States. Hammaker Car Rental Group is the parent of Avis Rent A Car and Budget Rent A Car.

Consultant to Ventrox, Branchville, New Jersey, to manage Ventrox's outsourced recruitment function, including developing processes, strategies, and uncovering recruiting sources. Candidates included senior-level Web Developers, Technical Architects, and Project Managers. Ventrox integrates online and offline marketing communications for the pharmaceutical industry.

Consultant to Jemin Holdings, Newark, Delaware, Washington, DC, and Atlantic City, New Jersey, to recruit technical, operational, and managerial candidates for all corporate locations. Worked with Jemin to evaluate current corporate recruitment processes and policies and made process improvement suggestions to its corporate task force. Evaluated Jemin's staffing vendors for effectiveness. Established recruiting resource relationships with colleges, Departments of Labor, and other organizations. Jemin Holdings is a 5,000-employee electric power provider and parent company to Connectiv and Atlantic City Electric.

Consultant to DKI Direct, Montvale, New Jersey, to manage DKI Direct's outsourced recruiting function, including developing processes and strategies and uncovering recruiting sources. Candidates included C# .NET and Java Web Developers, Senior Technical Architects with Microsoft technologies experience, Quality Assurance Manager, Project Manager, Data Manager, and Systems/Database Administrator. DKI develops online CRM and marketing programs for the pharmaceutical industry.

Consultant to Resolute Corporation, New York, New York and Philadelphia, Pennsylvania, to implement and improve recruiting processes, manage recruiting vendors, and support consulting practice growth in both markets. Candidates recruited included .NET Developers and Technical Architects using Microsoft technologies. Resolute is a consulting and IT services firm and a Microsoft Gold Partner.

Human Resources Resume Sample: Functional/Senior Manager, continued

Consultant to American Infrastructure, Malvern, Pennsylvania, to support growth in Pennsylvania, Delaware, Maryland, and Virginia. Responsibility was to recruit for field and corporate positions for all business units. Worked with senior management to develop a long-term proactive corporate recruiting strategy for company's seasonal staffing needs, to include processes and recruiting sources. American Infrastructure is a $365-million corporate parent to civil construction companies, a paving company, and a multiple-site/multiple-state construction materials supplier. American Infrastructure's companies include Independence Construction Materials and Allan A. Myers.

Project Manager as tier one sub-supplier to Sprint, Kansas City, Missouri. Managed recruiters and submittals for a 100 to 200-consultant-per-month project. Positions included hardware and software engineers for Sprint projects on a nationwide basis. Sprint is a $27 billion Fortune 100 telecommunications company.

Consultant to Electronic Data Systems (EDS), Des Moines, Iowa, to support growth projections in Iowa. Responsibility was to lead recruiting for two technical solutions centers in Des Moines and Cedar Rapids. EDS is a $20-billion Fortune 500 global technology solutions firm.

Consultant to General Dynamics Electronics Systems, Mountain View, California, to recruit C, C++, and Java Software Developers with Secret Security Clearances for government manufacturing projects located in Southern California. General Dynamics is a firm that provides information systems and technologies, land and expeditionary combat systems, armaments and munitions, shipbuilding and marine systems, and business aviation.

Consultant to Mikohn Gaming Corporation, Las Vegas, Nevada, to act as Recruiting Manager on a contract basis. Responsible for developing and implementing corporate recruiting strategies and practices for a new internal recruiting department. Responsible for all corporate departments, including Sales, Engineering, Game Development (software and hardware), IT, Call Center, Product Testing, and Executive Offices. Mikohn Gaming is a $96-million supplier of slot systems and casino gaming technology.

Consultant to Oracle Consulting, Los Angeles, California to recruit Oracle Technical and Functional Consultants for Oracle implementation projects on a nationwide basis. Oracle Corporation is the world's largest enterprise software firm.

Consultant to Cap Gemini Ernst & Young, El Segundo, California, as part of a team to support Ernst & Young's nationwide Oracle practice. Candidates included business development and functional and technical Oracle professionals at the Staff Consultant, Senior Consultant, Manager, and Senior Manager levels. Ernst & Young is a $14.5-billion tax, business, and technology consulting organization.

Human Resources Resume Sample: Functional/Senior Manager, continued

Consultant to Thinkspark Inc., Las Vegas, Nevada and Cleveland, Ohio, to establish internal recruiting departments for start-up consulting practices in both cities as well as support Thinkspark's national Oracle and Java education practice. Developed processes, strategies, and recruiting resources. Candidates recruited included Oracle Developer and DBA candidates, Java Developers, and Oracle and Java instructors. Thinkspark is a national Oracle education, product, and consulting partner.

Consultant to Ernst & Young, LLP, Dallas, Texas, to support Ernst & Young's new Business Transformation Synergy. Recruited Sales, Operations, and Sales Support Managers in the Telecom, IT, and Customer Support areas for practices nationwide. Ernst & Young is a $14.5-billion tax, business, and technology consulting organization.

Consultant to Andersen Consulting, Phoenix, Arizona, as Recruiting Project Leader supporting multiple large teams doing a Y2K conversion for customer American Express. Developed processes and procedures for the project, hired, managed, and trained contract recruiters assigned to the project, and provided projected management while maintaining personal production levels. Andersen Consulting, now called Accenture, is a $13.67-billion global management consulting, technology services, and outsourcing firm.

AFFILIATIONS

Society for Human Resource Management
Tri-State Human Resource Management Association
Recruitment Process Outsourcing Association
National Association of Personnel Services
National Association of Sales Professionals
United Way of Bucks County Community Investment Board

Information Technology Resume Sample: Chronological/Entry Level

Lisa Maskarich
e-mail lmaskarich@yahoo.com
650.743.4728 cell

Objective

Seeking early-stage career change to grow as an Information technology professional in Software and Hardware Technical Support, Desktop Support, Support Engineer, Systems Administration.

Professional Experience

SILICON VALLEY BANK, SANTA CLARA , CA   SEPT 2005 to JANUARY 2006
Senior Support
- Provided day-to-day end-user troubleshooting, resolved VPN connectivity issues, system and software deployment, new hire setups, disaster recover, asset management and tracking, hardware configuration, software configuration and imaging, warranty repair.
- Remote Administration, System Administration for servers, desktops, and laptops. Installed and supported over a hundred applications within the business infrastructure.
- Maintained Image and Operating System standards. Defined and documented operating system standard installation methods.
- Created and maintained application documentation one pagers.
- Installed hardware (e.g. RAM upgrades, Cisco VoIP, network cards, printers, and other peripherals).
- Supported and installed Windows (updates, patches, fixes).

Education

DE ANZA COLLEGE, CUPERTINO, CA 1994
Certificate of Completion for Business Applications
Certificate of Completion for Administrative Assistant

Information Technology Resume Sample: Chronological/Entry Level, continued

Technical Skills Summary

- Operating Systems: Windows 2000 Professional/XP, Windows 2000/2003 Server, and Windows 2003 Advanced Server.
- Hardware: Hewlett-Packard, Compaq, IBM, Dell, Toshiba, Sony, PDAs, and Clone systems.
- Software: MS Exchange, MS Office, MS Outlook, One Note, MS Project, Visio, Remedy, Clarify, Aperture, Track, Citrix, Shavlik, Oracle, SAP R/3, SQL Server, Adobe Acrobat Writer, Siebel, Peoplesoft, Hot Docs, FiServ Image Signature Verification, Equity Edge, Docutreev and WTR Client (Wire Workflow), Essbase, Moody's Financial Analyst, Business Objects, Photoshop, Illustrator, Quark, FrameMaker, McAfee, Symantec Anti-Virus, SMS, Ghost, PartitionMagic, and PCAnywhere.
- Networking/Internet: TCP/IP, NETBIOS, DHCP, WINS, DNS, SMTP, HTTP, FTP, IIS, Telnet, HTML, Cisco switches, 3Com switches, IE, and Netscape.

Certifications

- Microsoft Certified Professional Exams Successfully Completed:
  o Implementing and Supporting NT Server 4.0 in the Enterprise
  o Implementing and Supporting NT Server 4.0
  o Implementing and Supporting NT 4.0 Workstation
  o Networking Essentials
- A+ DOS/Win Certified Technician
- Compaq Certified for: Desktops, Laptops, Workstations, and ProLiant Servers

QuickStart Technical Training, San Jose, CA

- Networking Essentials
- Implementing and Supporting NT Server 4.0 in the Enterprise
- Implementing and Supporting NT Server 4.0
- Implementing and Supporting NT 4.0 Workstation
- Installing, Configuring, and Administering Microsoft® Windows 2000 Professional
- Implementing and Supporting Microsoft Exchange Server 5.5

Information Technology Resume Sample: Chronological/Individual Contributor

Sal R. Rhee
San Jose, CA 87759
(640) 879-9333
srr@comcast.net

SUMMARY PROFILE

Past-to-Present Desktop and Network Technology Service and Support

Over 20 years developing and deploying support tools and training for hardware and software products (legacy and new equipment)

Extensive IT site management and technical expertise (see Professional Experience below for details):

- Repairing, troubleshooting, and supporting 18,850 computer systems and their peripherals onsite and remote
- Deploying 16,470 new computer systems
- Resolving, documenting, and closing 4,250 trouble tickets
- High-level customer satisfaction and service
- Take-ownership attitude focused on customer satisfaction and issue resolution
- In-person and phone support interacting with end users, MIS managers, customers, and vendors
- Proven effective communicator with ability to build strong working relationships

PROFESSIONAL EXPERIENCE

Neighborhood Technology Specialist, San Carlos, CA   **Jan. 2004 to Present**
Owner – Part Time
- Technical support focused on local home and small business owners
- Supporting over 25 home and small business users
- Developed and deployed Microsoft Access data bases for local small businesses
- Specializing in configuring, securing, and maintaining wireless networks in homes and businesses
- Strong focus on removing and protecting systems from adware, spyware, viruses, worms, and Trojans

The High Note, San Leandro, CA   **Nov. 2005 to Present**
Sales Representative – Part Time
- Sale Representative supporting sales efforts of new and used musical instruments and their accessories
- Immediately established as the top Sales Representative for all three locations, with over $380,000 in sales to date

Information Technology Resume Sample: Chronological/Individual, continued

- Comfortable working across all departments within this retail store in both sales and support role of musical instruments and related accessories
- Working as the primary front counter support person and taking a majority of incoming calls to the store location
- Familiar with inventorying, setup, and pricing of musical instruments and their accessories for displaying on the retail floor

Chips 'R Us, Santa Clara, CA　　　　　　　　　　　　　**Apr. 1988 to Nov. 1996**
Technical Support Engineer
- Provided pre-sales technical support to customers on entire product line at Chips 'R Us Customer Information Call Center
- Liaison with peer engineers to resolve cross-organization integration issues
- Handled escalation calls for all CPO products, marketing promotions, and dealer programs, working with division contacts to resolve issues
- Coached 80 Product Technical Consultants on the First-Tier Help Desk in resolving customers' product and program issues
- Resolved, documented, and closed over 50,000 Second-Tier Help Desk customer calls, products and services
- Developed technical support tools and training for the launch of 45 new products
- Trained over 250 employees

Computer Attic, ComputerCraft, ComputerLand, San Jose-Sunnyvale-Santa Clara, CA
Repair Technician　　　　　　　　　　　　　　　　　　**Aug. 1983 to Mar. 1988**
- Designed and repaired computer systems and peripherals
- Consulted and designed computer and peripheral systems to best meet customer and sales rep needs
- Answered technical support line in service centers

Gonzo Video Game Corporation, Sunnyvale, CA　　　　**Apr. 1981 to Apr. 1983**
Lead Technician
- Troubleshot and repaired to component level company's line of game systems and computer systems and peripherals
- Worked closely with Automated Testing to help develop its code, which tested products
- Generated reports on most common failures for products

EDUCATION

Silicon Valley Tech, Diploma in Electronics, March 1981
Motherboard State University, Continuing Education in Internet and Computer Sciences
Service Authorizations from Apple, 3Com, Compaq, IBM
Ongoing personal development training programs

Information Technology Resume Sample: Chronological/Individual, continued

TECHNICAL EXPERTISE

PC Operating Systems
Windows XP, 2000, Me, 98se, 98, 95, 3.x, 2.x, 1.x. OS/2, MS DOS
Macintosh OS 10.x, 9.x, 8.x, 7.x, 6.x

Network Operating System
Windows Server 2003, Windows Server 2000, NT 4.0, NT 3.x
Mac OS X 10.x, Mac OS X Server 1.0, AppleShare IP, AppleTalk

Hardware
PCs and Laptops: Apple, Compaq, Dell, HP, Gateway, IBM, Toshiba, and generic clones
Peripheral Interfaces: HP-IB, HP-IR, IDE, Parallel, RS-232, RS-422, SATA, SCSI, USB
Mass Storage: Apple, Fujitsu, Hitachi, HP, IBM, Iomega, La Cie, Lexar, Maxtor, Memorex, Samsung, SansDisk, Seagate, Sony, Toshiba, WD
Printers: Apple, Epson, HP, IBM, Lexmark, QMS, Xerox

Networking
Hardware: 2Wire, 3Com, Cisco, D-Link, HP, Motorola, NetGear, Linksys, SMC
Protocols: DHCP, DNS, FTP, HTTP, IPX/SPX, SMTP, SNMP, Telnet, TCP/IP, AppleTalk, ATM, Ethernet, FDDI, Frame Relay, Token Ring, Wi-Fi

Software
Productivity: AppleWorks, Lotus Notes, Microsoft Office Suite
E-mail: ccMail, Eudora, Microsoft Outlook and Outlook Express
Internet Browser: AOL Explorer, Firefox, Internet Explorer, Mosaic, Netscape, Safari
Security: Ad-aware, McAfee, Spybot, Symantec, Windows Defender
Multimedia: Flash, RealAudio, Shockwave, QuickTime
Imaging: Acronis, Altiris, Dameware, Norton Ghost
Design: AutoCAD, Corel Draw, Illustrator, PageMaker, Photoshop

EXTRACURRICULAR ACTIVITIES

Usher, New World Amphitheater, Mountain Top, CA   **May 2006 to Present**
Assisting guests to their seats before and during the show
Ensure that the venue is ready before guests arrive for the show
Able to resolve difficult situations with guests using customer service skills
Maintain high standards for customer satisfaction at the show

Information Technology Resume Sample: Chronological/Manager

FRANK D. SCHUTCHEON
franks@yahoo.com
Office: (925) 965-7014
Cell: (925) 785-9225

OBJECTIVE

To obtain a growth-oriented Project or Program Manager role with a Fortune 500 software firm in the San Francisco Bay Area

---

PROFESSIONAL SUMMARY

A Human Resources Project / Program Manager with extensive experience business partnering with executive business sponsors, IT, end-user communities, and applications vendors to design and implement global, business-focused, total human capital strategies (talent acquisition/development, reward systems, HRIS).

- Strong business focus reinforced through dedicated experience as HRIT Project and Program Management in high-growth, industry-leading companies as well as own consulting firm.
- HRMS project management experience on both PeopleSoft through 8.9 (four projects) and Oracle through 11i (two projects).
- Significant time spent on-site internationally leading development of HRIT and compensation strategies and plans, particularly Japan, Taiwan, PRC, and UK.

PROFESSIONAL EXPERIENCE

FINICKY ASSOCIATES   **2002 – Present**

HRIT PROGRAM / PROJECT MANAGER

- Demonstrated ability to work with the management and internal IT team in a client company to strategize, select, and implement the right Human Resource information system to automate and optimally manage its human capital. The bottom-line outcome is to implement cost-effective, business-oriented human capital solutions to meet the company's needs.

Client companies include:

- Gotham Life Insurance of California (May 2006 – present) Program Manager working with HRIT to install the eComp module as part of PeopleSoft 8.9 HRMS.
- Endorse Support (October 2004 – November 2005) Acting HR/HRIT Manager to help drive HR initiatives in company, including upgrade to 8.9 PeopleSoft HRMS.

Information Technology Sample Resume: Chronological/Manager, continued

- Crabapple Computer (July – October 2005) Project/Program Manager to conduct vendor evaluation study of Oracle 11i vs. PeopleSoft 8.9.
- Tell-it-All Technology (January – June 2004) Project Manager to install Comp Workbench module on Oracle 11i HRMS.
- Pixie Dust (March – May 2003) Project Manager to conduct HRMS vendor evaluation/selection study – Erickson selected.
- Casual Communications (May – December 2002) Project Manager to complete a rapid (eight months) install of the PeopleSoft 8 version HRMS with core functionality to replace outdated PeopleSoft HRMS.

TACTILE TECHNOLOGY   **1999 – 2002**
PROGRAM/PROJECT MANAGER HRIT
- Led global development team of 100 to install Oracle 11i HRMS within two years ($45m+ project) – the first single-instance global install for the Oracle 11i system for all Oracle clients.

VISION QUEST INC.   **1996 – 1999**
DIRECTOR, COMPENSATION, BENEFITS, AND HRIS
- Helped take company from 120-employee start-up through IPO to 2,000 employees with a market cap of $16 billion.
- Business partnered with executive team to create company's HRIS strategy and select/install HRMS.
- Project Manager to successfully meet PeopleSoft HRMS rapid install (less than eight months) project plan.

APPLIED MATHEMATICS   **1992 – 1995**
DIRECTOR, GLOBAL COMPENSATION, BENEFITS, AND HRIS
- Lead international compensation/benefits team of 16 to develop and implement global total reward strategy (base, variable, sales, executive, benefits, stock, expatriate) and programs across 15 countries for a company of 6,000 employees.
- Team lead on compensation configuration for successfully installing global version of PeopleSoft HRMS in 10 countries.

Information Technology Resume Sample: Chronological/Manager, continued

EDUCATION

MS, University of Las Vegas, NV (with distinction); Major - Industrial Relations, Minor - Computer Science

BA, University of Athens, Greece; History

AREAS OF EXPERTISE

HRIT: PeopleSoft 8.9 (HRMS core, eCompensation, eCompManagerDesktop, HRMS Warehouse, Time & Labor, eProfile, Benefits Administration), Oracle 11i 10 (E-Business Suite modules for HR core, Self-Service Manager, Comp Workbench, Benefits, Time & Labor), Callidus (sales administrative support software), Ceridian (HR/payroll interface software).

PROJECT / PROGRAM MANAGEMENT: Accenture project manager training, Oracle University – E Business Suite training, Six Sigma, Waterfall sequential development management, Microsoft project methodology, executive level interaction and consensus building, Oracle Consulting project management methodology.

TYPES OF ENGAGEMENTS: Initial HRIT vendor analysis and comparison, new HRMS implementations, HRMS upgrades, module implementations, HR/Payroll interface installations, global HRMS implementations, sales compensation administration software implementations, acting role as HRIT program/project manager in consulting role.

Information Technology Resume Sample: Chronological/Senior Manager

N. Gene Near

Fremont, CA 98234

ngnear@gmail.com, (780) 146-0803

SUMMARY OF ACCOMPLISHMENTS

- Eight years of development experience in analysis, design, and development client/server applications involving storage technologies.
- Strong manager of diverse software development teams and applications processes
- Strong knowledge of storage system (volume manager, backup, disaster/recovery).
- Worked extensively on VERITAS Volume Manager.
- Worked extensively on Microsoft Volume Shadow Copy Service feature.
- Worked extensively on integration of VERITAS Volume Manager with VERITAS NetBackup.
- Ability to lead a group and make decisions on time.
- Extensive experience in developing, debugging multi-tier applications using VC++ and related technologies.
- Worked extensively on C++ with strong knowledge of OOPs.
- Sound knowledge of C.
- Good exposure to Windows internals.
- Strong debugging skills.
- Experience in using VISIO for class diagrams and sequence diagrams.
- Excellent analysis, documentation, and problem solving skills.
- Experience with full software development life cycle (SDLC) and the phases of the project life cycle.
- Good team player, ability to work within a team environment as well as independently.
- Strong interpersonal skills, with demonstrable verbal and written communication skills to maintain effective work relationships at all levels.

PROFESSIONAL EXPERIENCE

NetApp ONTAP Quality Assurance   **January 2006 – Current**

Project Lead

Network Appliance, Inc. (NetApp) is a world leader in unified storage solutions for today's data-intensive enterprise. Since its inception in 1992, Network Appliance has delivered technology and products that simplify data management. NetApp® storage solutions – which include specialized hardware, software, and services – provide seamless storage management for open network environments.

Information Technology Resume Sample: Chronological/Sr. Manager, continued

NetApp ONTAP Quality Assurance organization added bandwidth through an offshore engagement with Symphony Services to focus on quality improvements. There are three core areas that are outlining initial responsibilities within this document: WAFL, Protocols, and Data Protection (tape dump/restore, various snapmirror technologies).

Project Lead for the Data Protection Group/Protocols
Responsibilities:
- Managing the team of 10-15 members.
- Coordinating with offshore team.
- Understand the scope of deliverables.
- Developed the project plan to track the project at a granular level plan to successfully execute the project.
- Formulated test plans/test schedules with QA members.
- Lead the team for functional/regression/load tests.
- Lead and track schedule.
- Observe set processes as per operational plan and try to enhance it.
- Participate in team meetings.
- Review deliverables before delivering to client.
- Ensure that the deliverables meet with the client's acceptance criteria.

VERITAS   **June 1999 – January 2006**
Volume Manager
VERITAS (now known as Symantec Software) is a product-based company, mainly into data availability products. Volume Manager is an advanced version of LDM (Logical Disk Manager) that is bundled with all versions of Microsoft Windows 2000/XP. This product manages storage components like hardware arrays, provides functionality of Software RAID, multipathing, clustering support, snapshots support, storage organization, etc. This product is Microsoft Win2K Datacenter certified.

Participation in Features Design and Implementation in reverse chronological order:

VERITAS Volume Shadow Copy Service   **2003–2006 (VxSnap), 2001–2003 (vssprov)**
Sr. Software Engineer
Volume Shadow Copy Service (VSS) provides a three-way coordination among the Line of Business Applications (Writers), Backup Applications (Requestors), and Storage software (Providers) that owns the data that needs to be managed. VSS, which ships with Windows Server 2003, creates a point-in-time copy of volumes/files. Applications can continue to write data to the disk volume during the shadow copy process, which enables parallel online business and backup process.

Information Technology Resume Sample: Chronological/Sr. Manager, continued

Responsibilities:
* Key/primary developer for VSS Requestor (VxSnap) and was actively involved in all the phases of SDLC from concept to deployment.
* This requestor was developed using VC++.
* Played a major role in development of VSS S/W Provider (vssprov) for VERITAS VM and participated actively in all the phases from concept to deployment.
* This module was a Windows Service and was implemented in VC++.
* Responsible for the design and implementation of VxSnap integration with Microsoft Exchange.
* Was responsible for the design and implementation of the VxScheduler, a scheduling service for scheduling backups/restores using VxSnap and VSS.
* Implementing this module involved writing a Windows Service, a client module, and a server module. All these modules were implemented using VC++.
* Responsible for the design and implementation of the various features of the VxSnap, like snapshot creation, snapshot restore, log truncation, etc.
* VxSnap provided disaster recovery options for Exchange databases and hence enhanced the sales of the product significantly.
* Responsible for the design and implementation of vssprov, the integration component between VERITAS VM and Microsoft VSS.
* Vssprov made it possible for user to take snapshot/off-host backup of the dynamic volumes using VM's FlashSnap (FMR) feature and at the same time leverage Microsoft's VSS framework.
* Participated in business discussions and knowledge transfer activities as systems expert.
* Preparing low-level test plan for the QA team.
* Preparing the testing scenarios.
* Performing unit testing.
* Tracking the daily status of testing activities.
* Monitoring the defects logged and ensuring their timely resolution.
* Taking care of customer escalations actively.
* Responsible for version management and release of versions.

VERITAS Frozen Image   **2003 – 2006**
Senior Software Engineer
VERITAS has defined and implemented a library called VERITAS Frozen Image (VxFI), which is used to analyze possible frozen image methods or generate snapshot images of data objects. VxFI offers faster program development of a product by abstracting the stack elements throughout the storage environment. It hides the underlying structure of the storage management software stack from the application and lets application create frozen images. Frozen image of a volume, in simpler words, is snapshot or point-in-time copy of the original volume.

Information Technology Resume Sample: Chronological/Sr. Manager, continued

Responsibilities:
- Understanding the VxFI framework followed by the system analysis and then producing estimations.
- Designing and developing the application based on the requirements, documenting the requirement specifications.
- Preparing the high-level design and low-level design (document) of the entire application.
- Designing and developing the bridge between the VM and VxFI framework.
- This bridge was client module for VxFI and server module for the VM.
- This module was developed in VC++.
- Responsible for the design, development, and documentation of the complete module.
- Participated in business discussions and knowledge transfer activities as systems expert.
- Coordinating between VxFI and VM team.
- Preparing low-level test plan for the QA team.
- Preparing the testing scenarios.
- Performing unit testing.
- Tracking the daily status of testing activities.
- Monitoring the defects logged and ensuring their timely resolution.
- Responsible for version management and release of versions.

VERITAS Federated Mapping Service   2004 – 2006
Senior Software Engineer
VERITAS has defined and implemented a library called VERITAS Mapping Services (VxMS) to assist in the development of portable storage management applications. The services allow an application to determine information about files and volumes. It hides the underlying structure of the storage management software stack from the application. This feature is intended for enhanced integration between VERITAS VM and VERITAS NetBackup.

Responsibilities:
- Understanding the VxMS framework followed by the system analysis and then producing estimations.
- Designing and developing the application based on the requirements, documenting the system requirement specifications.
- Preparing the high-level design and low-level design of the entire application.
- Designing and developing the bridge between the VM and VxMS framework.
- This bridge was client module for VxMS and server module for the VM.
- This module was developed in VC++.
- Designing, development, and documentation of the complete module.
- Participated in business discussions and knowledge transfer activities as systems expert.

Information Technology Resume Sample: Chronological/Sr. Manager, continued

- Coordinating between VxMS and VM team.
- Preparing low-level test plan for the QA team.
- Preparing the testing scenarios.
- Performing unit testing.
- Tracking the daily status of testing activities.
- Monitoring the defects logged and ensuring their timely resolution.
- Responsible for version management and release of versions.

Dynamic Disk Group   **2000 – 2001**

Software Engineer

Dynamic Disk Group Split and Join (DGSJ) refers to two related commands – Split Dynamic Disk Group and Join Dynamic Disk Group (DG). Split DG splits a dynamic DG into two dynamic DGs, whereas Join DG joins two dynamic DGs into one merged DG. One can join two DGs that were originally split apart with the Split DG command, but one can also join two dynamic DGs that started out as separate DGs. This feature was mainly to aid user in reorganizing the dynamic DGs layout and take off-host backups.

Responsibilities:
- Understanding the ERD and MRD followed by the system analysis and then producing estimations.
- Designing and developing the application based on the requirements, documenting the system requirement specifications.
- Preparing the high-level design and low-level design of the entire application.
- Designing and developing server-side module and its client, i.e. CLI.
- Designing the GUI.
- This module was developed in VC++.
- Responsible for the design, development, and documentation of the complete module.
- Participated in business discussions and knowledge transfer activities as systems expert.
- Preparing low-level test plan for the QA team.
- Preparing the testing scenarios.
- Performing unit testing.
- Monitoring the defects logged and ensuring their timely resolution.
- Responsible for version management and release of versions.

Information Technology Resume Sample: Chronological/Sr. Manager, continued

EDUCATION

Masters in Computer Science (MCS), graduated in June 1999 with First Class with Distinction from N. Wadia College, Pune under University of Pune.

Bachelors in Computer Science (BCS), graduated in June 1997 with First Class with Distinction from H.A.L. College, Nashik under University of Pune.

TECHNICAL SKILLS

Operating Systems: Windows NT/2000/2003.

Programming Languages: C, C++.

Development Tools: Microsoft Visual Studio.

Technologies: Microsoft 2003 VSS, SDK programming, MFC, COM.

Tools/Applications: WinDbg, WinCVS, Microsoft Visual SourceSafe, VERITAS iTools, Microsoft Exchange 2003, WinInstaller.

Project Management: MS Office, Visio.

Domain: Storage (Volume Management, Clustering, FMR, MultiPathing, SAN)

Legal Resume Sample: Chronological/Entry Level

Frieda People
Phone: 815-786-0033
E-mail: legalgal@gmail.com

PROFILE

Full-time legal position. Bring, a wide variety of experience, and great research and writing skills.

EMPLOYMENT

Law Offices of Silverman & Silverman, LLP
Sept 2006-present
Immigration work including family-based petitions; PERM employment cases; research on immigration laws

Records Clerk, Hewey, Dewey, & Louey, LLP (Pathways Personnel)
Feb 2006-July 2006
Legal document review; analysis of litigation files; data entry in Elite

Legal Internship - Law Clerk, Law Office of Noah Terry Public
Jan 2005-May 2005
Research on criminal defense issues, drafting motions, meeting with clients in custody, court appearances, discovery

Legal Internship - Law Clerk, Regional Legal Aid
June 2004-Nov 2004
Client intake, research and writing, writing position statements, advocacy letters, welfare law, representation of clients at judicial hearings

Campaign Organizer, ACLU Racial Justice Project-Reform and Oversight
June 2003-Nov 2003
Voter outreach, fundraising, public speaking, advocacy on police issues

Program Associate, Advocates for Children and Youth
June 2000-Dec 2002
Event planner, special projects, administrative assistant, database and Web site manager

Legal Resume Sample: Chronological/Entry Level, continued

EDUCATION

Juris Doctorate, School of Law Practice, San Diego, California
Bachelor's of Arts, Political Science, State-of-the Art University, Vailsburg, Louisiana

COMPUTER SKILLS

Microsoft Office, database programs-Elite, Concordance, Adobe, word processing programs, Excel, Internet research using WestLaw and LexisNexis

LANGUAGES

Conversational Spanish

AWARDS

Foundation of the State Bar of California, Scholarship for excellence in public service

VOLUNTEER

Board of Directors, ACLU San Francisco Chapter

Legal Resume Sample: Functional/Individual Contributor

Dayon Knight
2975 Jackson Avenue
Houston, TX 77778
Knightcrawler@hotmail.com
(670) 5349-1089

Professional Summary

Business attorney and member of Texas Bar with broad range of experience, including:

- Plain language drafting and editing
- Factual and legal research and analysis
- Intellectual property and marketing support
- Contract negotiation and revision
- Risk management and compliance

Professional Highlights

Writing and Editing:

- Simplified insurance policy language to meet Department of Insurance readability standards
- Developed standard correspondence and corporate policies and procedures
- Reviewed and revised marketing materials, magazine and Web site copy, advertising, disclosures, manuals, programs, and procedures
- Prepared and revised pleadings and exhibits for filing
- Established standards for Spanish-language translations
- Compiled and reconciled internal style guides

Risk Management and Compliance:

- Reviewed travel law and operations, devised preventive law program, and advised on legal issues and member claims
- Implemented workplace injury prevention and right-to-know programs, advised on OSHA and environmental compliance, and helped train managers
- Revised company driver improvement program
- Managed contract aspects of personal computer network rollout

Legal Resume Sample: Functional/Individual Contributor, continued

Intellectual Property and Marketing:

- Established and managed the intellectual property program, including screening and registering trademarks and copyrights, maintaining trade secret and privacy protection
- Reviewed basic patent questions and use of outside counsel
- Coordinated TSAA marketing with AAA national policies
- Proofed and corrected insurance advertising, magazine copy, and marketing materials

Contract Negotiation and Revision:

- Negotiated software licenses, information technology project agreements, contractor service agreements, nondisclosure agreements, and other contracts
- Reviewed and negotiated HMO mandates and enrollment agreements
- Developed contract review policies and form contracts

Employee Training:

- Trained employees in ethics, OSHA compliance, and other basic legal issues
- Reviewed online and printed training materials
- Coached TSAA and Toastmasters clubs

Legislative Analysis:

- Advised governmental affairs staff on proposed Texas legislation
- Established compliance with legislation as enacted and regulations as adopted

Litigation:

- Litigated and arbitrated property damage, personal injury, and insurance claims
- Participated in discovery, document review and production, and witness appearances
- Represented TSAA in administrative hearings

Employment

Texas State Automobile Association (TSAA), Office of the General Counsel:
Senior Counsel, 2003-2005; Attorney I through III, 1976-2003:
Performed legal research, reviewed and approved all types of copy for publication, drafted and approved company employment and business policies, revised contract and insurance policy language, resolved intellectual property questions, reviewed and managed travel and insurance questions and claims, advised on workplace safety questions, and reviewed legislation.

Legal Resume Sample: Functional/Individual Contributor, continued

Texas Gas Transmission:
Legal assistant, summarized pipeline hearing transcripts

Bender, Arm, & Howe, LLP:
Editorial assistant, real estate transactions, for Texas Legal Forms

Fall, Guy & Associates:
Researcher, Judicial Council Master-Individual Calendar Study N

U.S. Navy:
Photographic electronic control systems technician

Volunteer Professional Activities

- Editorial staff of local bar publications
- Judicial arbitrator, Dallas Superior Court
- Attorney-client fee dispute arbitrator, Bar Association of Dallas
- Lemon law arbitrator, Dallas Better Business Bureau
- Member, ethics committee and intellectual property section
- Delegate, Texas State Bar Conference of Delegates

Education

- University of Texas at El Paso, College of Law: American Jurisprudence Award, J.D.
- Yale University: B.A., magna cum laude, with honors in Latin American Studies

Community and Educational Activities

- Dallas Unified School District, substitute teacher
- Dallas Museum of Texas Docent Program
- Yale University Summer Internship and Alumni Schools Committees
- Toastmasters International
- Coast Guard Auxiliary

Legal Resume Sample: Chronological/Manager

Jack Frost
12 Fast-Freeze Lane
Nome, AK 99762
907-944-3298
letitsnow@earthlink.net

SUMMARY

Former Assistant District Attorney for Seattle, currently serving as a Foreign Service Officer (U.S. Department of State), expert in managing teams in immigration law with extensive trial experience, seeks to enter private practice with an established firm or company.

PROFESSIONAL EXPERIENCE

U.S. Department of State, Washington D.C., London, UK and Juarez, Mexico.
Foreign Service Officer/Vice Consul/Manager
June 2004 – Present

- Interpret the Immigration and Nationality Act, the Foreign Affairs Manual, case law, and other internal guidance in the adjudication of non-immigrant and immigrant visas with an emphasis on petition-based visas.
- Develop an extensive understanding of international criminal and immigration laws as applied in immigrant and non-immigrant cases with criminal records, previous immigration violations or medical conditions.
- Draft Congressional correspondence requests and interagency legal memoranda.
- Advocate U.S. foreign policy and manage legal teams to bolster American businesses through international relations.
- Facilitate international summits, meetings, and informal gatherings in a diplomatic capacity.
- Interact with U.S. Congressional, Judicial, and Executive offices in managing and coordination of international conferences and visits.
- Assist American citizens abroad in a variety of situations ranging from adoption to arrests.

Office of the District Attorney, Seattle, WA
Assistant District Attorney
April 2001 – June 2004

- Litigated over 20 jury trials in a wide variety of criminal cases, with extensive experience in the prosecution of domestic violence and crimes against women and children.
- Experienced in all aspects of trial work, including pretrial motions, voir dire, examination of expert and lay witnesses, evidentiary issues, and argument.

Legal Resume Sample: Chronological/Manager, continued

- Enjoyed strong relationships with the bench and employed successful negotiating techniques with opposing counsel.
- Acted as a community liaison manager on behalf of the Office with local business leaders and constituents.
- Coordinated certified summer interns, critiquing and editing research and writing projects and supervising court appearances.

INTERNSHIPS
- Office of the District Attorney, San Francisco, CA
  Spring 2000
- Office of the District Attorney, San Diego, CA
  Summer 1999
- Legal Aid Compton, Compton, CA
  Summer 1998

EDUCATION
- Yale Law School, New Haven, CT, JD, May 2000
  Loyola Scholar (full scholarship)
  Member Black Law Students Association
- University of Southern California, AB, English Literature, May 1997

PROFESSIONAL ASSOCIATIONS AND CLEARANCES
- California State Bar Association
- Charles Hamilton Houston Bar Association
- Security Clearance, Top Secret

LANGUAGES
- Spanish and Italian

Legal Resume Sample: Chronological/Senior Manager

SHARON SHARALIKE
679 Paxson Road
San Bernardino, CA 97821
Cell: (410) 111-8767; Phone (410) 557-3101
E-mail: sharonsharalike@comcast.net

SUMMARY:

Experienced real estate transactional attorney with large law firm management experience in commercial litigation and seven years as lead real estate transactional attorney for Richenpoor's law firm. Looking for an in-house or law firm position as a real estate management transactional attorney.

PROFESSIONAL EXPERIENCE:

MARCH 2005 – JULY 2005

Abbott & Costello, Flagstaff, Arizona

Real Estate Transactional Attorney

Reviewed, revised, managed, and provided advice on: commercial leases, including office, retail and hotel space; unimproved and improved property sales representing sellers and buyers; and parking and emergency access easements. Closed several deals, including a $28-million condominium sale in Hawaii involving three escrows. Second attorney on a $100-million, six-hotel portfolio sale to Credit Suisse First Boston.

2001-PRESENT

Richenpoor Utility Company, Los Angeles, California

Lead Real Estate Transactional and Political Law Compliance Attorney

Lead real estate transactional attorney for one of the largest private employers and landowners in California:

- Provide day-to-day advice and counsel on all real estate matters for Richenpoor's entire service territory from Bakersfield to the California/Oregon border.

- Supervise and manage all (i) surplus property sales of $60+ million portfolio; (ii) leasing of third-party property, including office and industrial space, totaling over one million square feet; (iii) third-party uses of Richenpoor's property, including leases, licenses, and easements, and (iv) streetlight and other distribution facilities sales.

- Handle more than 50 transactions at a time and regularly advise/manage six Richenpoor departments.

Legal Resume Sample: Chronological/Senior Manager, continued

- Draft and update all form agreements, including purchase and sale agreements, leases (both tenant and landlord-oriented), licenses, and easements associated with practice area in conjunction with Corporate Real Estate (CRE) and outside counsel.

- Experienced with complex transactions involving environmental cleanups, environmental mitigation, Subdivision Map Act issues, condemnation, and California Public Utilities Commission regulatory compliance issues.

- Provide full-day biannual training to regional CRE personnel on new procedures and form agreements.

- Drafted, in conjunction with CRE and outside counsel, a comprehensive leasing manual providing detailed, step-by-step instructions on how to lease property as a tenant from the time that a need for leased space is identified through lease termination and exiting of the premises.

- Lead real estate in-house liaison to Richenpoor's outside counsel during Chapter 11 reorganization.

- Supervise and manage all outside counsel firms supporting Richenpoor's real estate practice, including all associated administrative responsibilities of hiring contracts, budgets, and bill review and approval.

- Sole in-house political law compliance attorney for multibillion-dollar regulated utility:

- Advise, in conjunction with outside counsel, on all lobbying, gift-giving, in-kind contribution and campaign activities, and associated required internal and external reporting of those activities and conflict of interest issues related to the above.

- Provide formal annual training tailored to each client department.

- Supervise outside counsel, review and approve all billings, and manage associated budgets and contracts.

1997–2000
Richenpoor Utility Company, Los Angeles, California
Real Estate/Corporate Transactional and Political Law Compliance Attorney
Supervise and manage all surplus property sales and large office and industrial leases in which Richenpoor is a tenant. Negotiate and draft wide variety of corporate agreements (approximately 75 total) including: construction of facilities, including transmission towers, underground transmission lines and warehouse complex; software licensing; energy efficiency programs; telecommunication installations; cleanup and transport of hazardous and nuclear waste; environmental and business consulting; and replacement security system for nuclear power plant. Author of Richenpoor's Uniform Standard Practice of Law Department Requirements Concerning Contracting, setting forth companywide requirements for negotiating, drafting, and executing corporate transactions. Sole in-house political law compliance attorney performing duties described above.

Legal Resume Sample: Chronological/Senior Manager, continued

1996–1997
Tweedledee & Tweedledum, LLC, Santa Barbara, California
Litigation and Transactional Attorney practicing in the areas of real estate, banking, public finance, and bankruptcy.

1993–1996
P. Yore & Cympull, Emeryville, California
Business consultant to several businesses developing and marketing portable water purification systems to Africa and India while starting up own gourmet coffee cart business, Bean Me Up, at the Oakland International Airport.

1990–1993
Schake, Wraddle & Rolle, San Francisco, California
Litigation Associate in general commercial practice group.

EDUCATION:
Harpo Marx School of Law, University of California, Santa Cruz, 1990
B.A., English Literature, University of California, Santa Cruz, 1986
Magna Cum Laude
Phi Beta Kappa
Not for Profit

Education Resume Sample: Chronological/Entry Level

Teaching Assistant

Dinah Myte
374 84th Street, New York, NY
(718) 650-1170, dmyte@earthlink.net

OBJECTIVE:
Teacher Assistant with a commitment to providing productive teaching that promotes child development.

EXPERIENCE:

2006–Present
RIVERDALE PRESCHOOL
Teacher Assistant – Assisting the teacher with all activities regarding the classroom and the children.

2005–2006
EAST SIDE FOUNDATION DAY CARE
Teacher Assistant – Assisted the teacher with children in classroom. I worked alongside the Teacher, creating lesson plans and other activities for the children.

2004–2005
JP MORGAN CHASE BANK
Client Associate – Interacted with the public to assist customers with their banking transactions, inform them about company products and services, and refer them to appropriate staff for further assistance.

2000--004
MANHATTAN NEW SCHOOL (PUBLIC SCHOOL 290)
Teacher Assistant – Assisted teachers during an after-school program. Watched over children and engaged in activities with them.

ADDITIONAL SKILLS:
Experienced with Macintosh Computers, (OS 9 up to recent). Worked with Internet Explorer, Safari, Microsoft Word, and PowerPoint.

EDUCATION:
ROSEMONT COLLEGE, NEW YORK, NY
B.A., History
Relevant Courses: Special Issues for Secondary Schools, African-American History, Latin American to 1825, 20th Century Europe

Education Resume Sample: Chronological/Individual Contributor

Educator, Private Tutor

KENNY WOURKE
818 Durbin Ave, Apt 11
Dallas, TX 75223
469-554-2637
Dallasdude@hotmail.com

OBJECTIVE:

To obtain part-time, supplemental work as an educator or private tutor of children or adults in a place of learning dedicated to the development of people into more loving, socially active, and creative individuals. Open to full-time, live-in appointments.

EMPLOYMENT:

Adjunct Psychology Instructor   **2005–2007**
US Navy/Central Texas College, TX
Deploy around the world enrolling, counseling, and teaching psychology and other university courses to military personnel at sea.

Special Education Teacher   **2003–2004**
Ridgemont Middle School—GISD, TX
Taught sixth through eighth grade content mastery and English resource.

Part-Time Employment   **1995–2003**
Various Texas institutions
Adjunct faculty (East Texas State College)
After-school tutor (Johnson Learning Center)
Substitute teacher (Eastwood School and Rock Hill Academy)
Assistant librarian (University of Texas at El Paso)
Academic tutor (Steadman Academy)
Substitute teacher (Wayburn High School)

Education Resume Sample: Chronological/Individual Contributor, continued

EDUCATION:

June 2003—Master of Education in Human Development and Psychology
Harvard University; Cambridge, Massachusetts

May 2001– Bachelor of Arts in History
University of the Ozarks; Clarksville, Arkansas

PROFESSIONAL DEVELOPMENT:

Teacher Certified in History and Special Education
Texas State Board of Education Member
Queen's University of Belfast, teaching scholarship; Northern Ireland, UK

VOLUNTEER WORK:

Delivered food to the homeless at First Church of Cambridge Congregational, Cambridge, Massachusetts (2002-03); Tutored and mentored youth from low-income backgrounds at the Wilkinson Center's Summer Safe Haven Program in Dallas, Texas (2004-05); Taught fifth and eighth grade Sunday school and Vacation Bible School at Spring Creek Community Church in Garland, Texas (2002-04); mentored children with disabilities and their siblings at Camp Discovery in McKinney, Texas (2002-03); Provided after-school childcare and tutored college students at the University of the Ozarks in Clarksville, Arkansas (2000); Led middle/high school Bible study during summer camps at Louisiana Tech and Stephen F. Austin Universities (1999-04).

AWARDS AND AFFILIATIONS:

All-American and Irish-American Scholar (2001-2002); Ozarks Area Theological Society (2000-Present); National Dean's List; Alpha Chi (2000); Phi Alpha Theta (2000); Rotaract (2000); Co-founder of the Human Development and Psychology Club at Harvard's Graduate School of Education and Graduate Chancellor's List (2003).

REFERENCES:

Provided upon request

Education Resume Sample: Chronological/Manager

Educational Director
Wanda Teech
2395 Franklin Parkway, Philadelphia, PA 98552
(470) 988-5050 (cell), Tiech.wanda@paymca.org

OBJECTIVE:
To obtain a position coordinating and directing educational programs, with a focus on sustainability education and curriculum development.

WORK HISTORY:
Unit Leader
YMCA of Greater Seattle, Seattle, WA   **2006**
- Coordinated, planned, and implemented programs for a summer day camp
- Organized and arranged field trips
- Maintained records and documented unit activities
- Supervised counselors and enforced safety procedures
- Communicated with parents, staff, and children
- Acted as director of ancillary program with responsibility for curriculum, supervision, and purchasing of materials

Outdoor Science Education Coordinator
Camp Highland Outdoor Science School, Cherry Valley, CA   **2005**
- Led, planned, and developed curriculum, classes, and activities for school groups grades 4-7
- Taught courses in geology, watershed, native skills, plants, tracking, orienteering, weather, birding, invertebrates, ecology, environmental action, plants, rock climbing, canoeing, archery, teambuilding, and low ropes
- Facilitated large group activities, for 15 students, with a focus on recreational, life skills, hiking, and daytime/ nighttime activities
- Enforced safety procedures and behavioral expectations in accordance with Camp Highland regulations
- Maintained, improved, and repaired grounds and facility set-up

Naturalist (Intern)
Aldo Leopold Nature Center, Madison, WI   **2004**
- Taught experiential education classes throughout the summer camp season
- Assisted the director and registrar in the coordination of school tours, day programs, summer camps, and public programs
- Organized materials and camp mailings for science-based day camps

Education Resume Sample: Chronological/Manager, continued

Research Assistant
University of Wisconsin, Madison, WI   12/03–8/04
* Worked with professor testing local pollen samples
* Analyzed pollen archives and created database
* Researched climatic change reports for scientific journal article by professor

Geography Library Assistant
University of Wisconsin, Madison, WI   09/03–05/12/03
* Assisted library patrons in finding materials and using library circulation system

Recreation Technician
Tahoe National Forest, Nevada City, CA   06–08/03
* Instructed public visitors on correct usage of the national lands
* Maintained campgrounds, recreation areas, and ATV sites
* Worked on construction projects such as rebuilding of fire rings and clearing of lumber
* Cleared trails and participated in owl and wildlife sightings
* Operated four-wheel-drive vehicle in very rugged terrain

EDUCATION:
* University of Wisconsin, B.A. – Geography and Spanish, May 2003
* Pontificia Universidad Católica de Chile – Spanish culture and immersion, June 2001
* Bronx High School of Science – Bronx, NY, June 1999

ADDITIONAL EXPERIENCE:
* Appalachian Mountain Club: Blairstown, NJ. Assisted in daily operations of a hiker lodge, including organization and planning of weekly activities, 2002.
* Camp Ramaquoius: Pomona, NY. Climbing wall instructor for a day camp, 2001.
* Appalachian Mountain Club: Lanesboro, MA. Cooked meals for a hiker lodge, assisted in daily chores, and maintained camping supplies store, 2000.
* Volunteered as English teacher to young children in Santiago, Chile.
* Took advanced Spanish literature and language classes throughout college.
* First Aid and CPR-certified.

References furnished upon request

Education Resume Sample: Chronological/Senior Manager

Athletic Director

Armin Hammer, Jr.
202 Charles Street
Winston, MA 90881
Phone 677-804-2552
E-mail: ahammer@pumpu.edu

OBJECTIVE:

Highly accomplished Athletic Director seeking Department Operations Head role with a growth-motivated NCAA, Division III College Program

EXPERIENCE:

2002-Present
Pump University, Boston, MA
Assistant Director of Athletic Facilities

- Supervise and monitor all NCAA Division III athletic events, AAU tournaments, Special Olympics tournaments, and any other outside contests held at the university. Responsibilities include tickets, setup, breakdown, crowd management, student-worker management, and overall event management.
- Apply my organizational skills to support the Athletic Center in all facets of department activities, including duties related to the efficient functioning of the Athletic Center and intramural and recreational sports.
- Administer, hire, and supervise facility staff, as well as student workers.
- Market and advertise varsity athletic, intramurals, club sports, and all other programs/events in the Athletic Center.
- Perform sports information duties as they relate to club sports, football, and softball, including writing stories, calculating statistics, photographs, and special releases.
- Use my strong supervisory, management, and communication skills in organizing athletic and recreational events, enabling me to develop a positive rapport with both staff and students.
- Collaborate weekend programming in coordination with intramural and recreational activities, focusing on one- or two-day tournaments targeting campuswide involvement.
- Provide help with club sport supervision and programming.

Education Resume Sample: Chronological/Senior Manager, continued

2000–2002
Grayson College, Lowell, MA
Department of Athletics
Assistant Football Coach
Assistant Softball Coach
- Recruited prospective student-athletes, working with the Office of Admissions, including attendance at numerous college fairs, open houses, and high schools as well as meeting with prospective student-athletes and their families for on-campus visits.
- Partnered with head coach to plan and implement daily practice and game activities.
- Knowledge and implementation of NCAA Division III rules and procedures.
- Participated in Athletic Department responsibilities, including monitoring student-athlete progress.
- Represented the Athletic Department at open houses and collegewide events.
- Worked in partnership with the Commonwealth Coast Conference and the New England Football Conference concerning league statistics.
- Collaborated with Athletic Department staff in fundraising activities.
- Coordinated team travel plans.
- Coordinated NCAA merchandise for post-season events.

1998–2000
Harris High School, Harris, MA
Department of Athletics
Game Manager
- Game manager/supervisor for home hockey games.
- Supervised and monitored school athletic events in coordination with Massachusetts Interscholastic Athletic Association rules.
- Handled ticket taking, security, meeting and greeting visiting teams and officials, and overall supervision of the athletic event.

EDUCATION:

2003–2005
Master of Education in Organizational Management
Swooton College, Westford, MA

1999–2003
Bachelor of Arts in History
University of Massachusetts-Dartmouth, North Dartmouth, MA

Education Resume Sample: Chronological/Senior Manager, continued

ADDITIONAL COACHING CREDENTIALS:

- Coordinated practice and game activities for the Bay State Summer Games while serving as the Head Coach in the 2005 and 2006 Summer Games and Assistant Coach in 2004.
- Four years' coaching at the North Shore Football Camp.
- Special Olympics track coach for the Massachusetts Special Olympic program.
- New Bedford Massachusetts Public School System Substitute Teacher, Tutor, and Referee, 2000-2002.
- Taught at the junior and senior high school levels as a substitute teacher. In addition, refereed basketball games for the New Bedford area middle schools.
- Provided after-school programs, allowing me to work with academically troubled students.

CERTIFICATIONS/LICENSURES:

7/22/2006
Massachusetts Test for Educator Licensure
Communication and Literacy Skills
Massachusetts Department of Education, MA

12/13/2005
CPR/AED Certification
American Red Cross, ARC of New England, Dedham, MA

12/13/2005
First Aid Certification
American Red Cross, ARC of New England, Dedham, MA

05/2003
Coaching Certification
Leeman College, Andover, MA

Arts Resume Sample: Chronological/Entry Level

Art Photography Manager

Art Luhvor
New York, NY
altruistic_photography@yahoo.com
www.flickr.com/photos/altruistic_photography

OBJECTIVE

To gain experience working in art, photographic, and journalistic settings for a nonprofit organization and/or museum/gallery. To use initiative when working with innovative technologies and motivated people. To interact and explore possibilities of ideas with colleagues in a contemporary photography/art/journalism setting.

EXPERIENCE

Freelance Writer and Editor
NY Museums Magazine, New York, NY   **July 2005 – Present**
Collating articles from small team of writers, editing for content.
Writing articles concerning artists, galleries, and other artistic concerns.
Published in print and online at www.nymuseums.org.

Intern
People's Gallery, New York, NY   **June 2005 – July 2005**
Working as a gallery assistant within a small gallery located on Broadway.
Hosting gallery openings and events. Showing pieces in gallery to visitors.
Answering phones and giving out gallery information.
peoplesgallerynyc.com

Photographer's Assistant
Paul Byrd, Photographer   **September 2004 – July 2006**
Working as an assistant to studio and location photographer Paul Byrd.
General assisting responsibilities, setting up lighting and backdrops. Arranging cameras, film, digital storage.

Arts Resume Sample: Chronological/Entry Level, continued

EDUCATION
Birmingham University, Liverpool, England
BA (Hons), Documentary and Fine Art Photography, June 2004
Part of group exhibition: INFUSION at Cube Gallery, Manchester, England.
(www.infusion-photo.com)

SKILLS
Monochrome Photography
Monochrome Darkroom
Color Photography
Color Darkroom
Digital Photography
Film Photography
SLR / Medium / Large Format Camera Systems
Studio Setup
Studio Flash
On Camera Flash

Macintosh OSX
Windows 95/98/XP
Abode Photoshop
Adobe InDesign
Adobe Image Ready
Adobe Acrobat
Microsoft Office
Internet
Scanning (Epson Perfection/Expression, Nikon Cool Scan Software)

PUBLISHED ARTICLES
Non-Profit or Non-Attending? Today's Museum Funding Crisis
NY Museums Magazine, Issue 10 – September/October 2005

Converging Funding Priorities at Columbus Museum of Art
NY Museums Magazine, Issue 11 – November/December 2005

Art or Endowment: Which Will Go First?
NY Museums Magazine, Issue 5 – May/June 2006

Arts Resume Sample: Functional/Individual Contributor

Art Gallery Curator

Rich Media
388 10th Avenue
New York, NY 11215
518-780-7709
rich.media@hotmail.com

OBJECTIVE

Become a gallery/museum assistant or similar role in other nonprofit organization in the fine arts field.

WORK HIGHLIGHTS

Graduate of Pratt Institute with a painting major. Award-winning artist expert in numerous media, including oils, watercolors, acrylics, and pen and ink. Successfully design and build museum displays of portraits, landscapes, and still life paintings as well as ceramics and fiber and glass arts.

WORK HISTORY

2004–2007:
Gallery Director Assistant, Walter Sanders Gallery, Chelsea, New York
Gallery Curation/Administration, Gallery Vietnam, Tribeca, New York
Participating in Toronto Art Fair
Participating in Art Miami
English teacher assistant tutoring, Incheon, Korea

EDUCATION

BFA, PRATT Institute, Brooklyn, NY, United States, 2004
Art Certificate, St. John's University, Jamaica, NY, United States, 2001

Arts Resume Sample: Functional/Individual Contributor, continued

---

AWARDS

Guildford Museum, Art Show Award, New York, 2002
Guildford Museum, Certificate of Recognition - Style Award, New York, 2003
Johnston Gallery, Outstanding Artistic Achievement, New York, 2004
Johnston Gallery, New Artist Recognition Award, New York, 2004

EXHIBITIONS

United States
East Hall Gallery at Pratt, Brooklyn, NY, 2006
Painting Group Show at Schaffer Gallery at Pratt Institute, Brooklyn, NY, 2006
Fine Arts Exhibition at Sun-Yat-Sen Gallery at St. John's University, Jamaica, NY, 2004

Canada
Open Studio Exhibition Art Show, Surrey, BC, 2002

TECHNICAL SKILLS

MS Word, Photoshop, Illustrator, QuarkXpress, PowerPoint, Excel.

Arts Resume Sample: Chronological/Manager

ART EXHIBITIONS MANAGER

Carole Inge
980 Upton Street, Apt. 12H
Cincinnati, OH 45202
513-814-658

OBJECTIVE

To manage teams doing innovative work that makes a difference in people's lives while providing me new knowledge and skills. Seek opportunities to use my creative talents, boundless energy, and practical skills in order to give back to the world. Expect to work with a nonprofit organization working with young people and/or art (visual), passionate about using skills and talents to work for the common good.

RELEVANT WORK EXPERIENCE

Non-Profit Manager / August 2005–Present
Anderson Heritage Center, Cincinnati, OH
This was a position through Urban Appalachian Council's AmeriCorps program through which I wrote grants, developed, managed and led community arts projects, held fundraisers, recruited and managed volunteers, and managed office and community room rentals.

Project Manager Assistant / January–July 2005
Pan Center for Intercultural Arts, Dayton, OH
I provided administrative support for arts-for-social-change projects, assisted in workshops, developed a teacher's resource pack to accompany workshops, and supplied a vital link between fieldwork and the office, gaining experience in working with schools, press, funding bodies and youth centers, grant applications, budgets, database entry, accounts, and evaluation/monitoring.

Gallery and Department Assistant / August 2000–May 2004
Dayton University, Department of Art, Cincinnati, OH
I assisted the gallery director in hanging art exhibitions. I also facilitated art exhibition openings and provided assistance to the Art Department as needed.

Arts Resume Sample: Chronological/Manager, continued

Artist Assistant / June–July 2000
Convergence 2000 (fiber arts conference), Cincinnati, OH
I was a part of a team of five people who volunteered to help professional artist Jane Dougherty create a large-scale installation in the Givens Center's Art Gallery.

Model Assistant / October 1999–June 2000
Cincinnati Museum Center, Cincinnati, OH
I volunteered eight hours a week to work with a team of people to create the permanent exhibit, "Cincinnati in Motion."

EDUCATION
City University London, London, England / 2004
Postgraduate Diploma in Cultural Management
The modules covered include Education and the Arts, Management, Managing People, Cultural Framework, Marketing, Finance, Fundraising, and a semester internship.

University of Dayton, Dayton, OH / 1998–2002
Bachelor's in Fine Arts Degree with a Concentration in Sculpture
Minor in Women and Minorities Studies

CURRENT AFFILIATIONS
Monfort Heritage Center – Board Member, Volunteer
Creative Cottage – Co-chair of Art Show Fundraiser
Greater Cincinnati YMCA – Member
Pan Center for Intercultural Arts – Volunteer, Partner Organization
Urban Appalachian Council – Partner Organization
East End Community Heritage School – Partner Organization
Cincinnati Recreation Commission – Partner Organization

COMPUTER SKILLS
Proficient in Microsoft Word, PowerPoint, Excel, and Outlook
Familiar with Microsoft Publisher and Access
Basic skills in Macromedia Fireworks
Type 60 words per minute

Arts Resume Sample: Functional/Senior Manager

PUBLIC TV PRODUCER/DIRECTOR

Ray Tings
78 Lake Shore Drive
Chicago, IL 60675
312-927-3545
tings@foreverfilms.com

CAREER HIGHLIGHTS

Conception through Distribution. Features, Live Action, National Television, Animation, News, Live Broadcasts, Streaming Media, Educational Series. Mobile Entertainment. Video Games. Talk Shows. Film, Digital Video, HD, Script Writing, Research, Line Producing, Field Producing, Directing, VO Direction, Post Production Supervisor, Videographer, Nonlinear Editing, Interactive Projects, DVD Authoring, Proposal Writing, Budget Writing. Managing crews and talent. Technical Training, Publicity, Press Releases, Script Breakdowns, Hiring of freelance crews and field producers. Negotiation for royalties and contract writing, Mediator, Advisor. Managing and researching broadcast rights and stock footage, Fundraising, International co-productions; including Eurimage. Post Conflict and Conflict environments. Scheduling to ensure deadlines are met. Quality and Budget controller. Union and Non-Union Productions. International experience. Award Winning.

PBS TV 2006-2007
Production Manager
Reality Show "Taxi Cab Confessions," Chicago, IL. First episode and all prep. Airing now.

VP VIDEO 2005
Producer
John Frederickson Strategic Media Company, based in San Pablo, California. Developed and produced nonprofit television series, documentaries, educational series, and news programs. Managed and hired a staff that included two producers, two researchers, and two editors with three post-production facilities. Managed business development and educational programs for the entire company.

LOLA DA MUSICA 2004
Executive Producer
Multi award-winning music series for National Television. Film/Digital Video. Multiple cameras. Winner: "Best Music Series in Europe" 2004

Arts Resume Sample: Functional/Senior Manager, continued

WINTER OLYMPICS 2002-2004
Producer, Director, Editor
Created over 40 motion pictures in less than 25 days during the 2002 Winter Olympics in Utah, for Coca-Cola. Built a nonlinear editing facility on location in Park City. Videotaped and conducted interviews. Encoded and tested all movies for webcasting. Managed and trained staff and production crew.

TWEEK CITY 2002
Producer, Line Producer
Feature Film directed by Eric Johnson. Starring Giuseppe Andrews, Keith Brunsmann, and Demetrius Navarro. Filmed on Location in Los Angeles, San Francisco, and Sacramento.

WISHED ON THE MOON 2001
Producer, Director, Editor
Feature Production based on a selection of Dorothy Parker short stories.

LOS LOBOS 2001
Producer, Director
Created a "Behind the Scenes" Documentary for the November 9, 2001 DVD release of the Los Lobos concert "Live at the Fillmore."

ELECTRONIC ARTS 2000
Producer, Director, and Editor
Short animated piece illustrating the fantastic environments for UXO, the latest version of their popular video game ULTIMA.

FIFTY CROWS MEDIA 1999
Director, Editor
Series of short movies based on the photo essays of the Documentary Photography Award Winners. Produced by Andy Patrick. Fifty Crows Media and Link TV.

MUSEUM OF AFRICAN DIASPORA 1998
Museum Curator
Curated images for the four movies on the main floor of the Museum; "Origins of Man" Expressionistic. Part of the museum's permanent collection. Researched, negotiated licenses and fees. www.moadsf.org Museum Collection.

Arts Resume Sample: Functional/Senior Manager, continued

BOYS CLUB OF NEW YORK 1998
Executive Producer, Camera
Documentary series about children living in New York City (Harlem). National Television.

SUMMER CHILDREN 1997
Executive Producer
Six-part reportage series about children and their summer activities. National Television Series.

OUR KINGDOM IN TWELVE CHAPTERS 1996
Executive Producer
12-part series, illustrating daily life and historical tales about each of the 12 provinces in The Netherlands. National Television Series.

THE CALENDAR 1995
Executive Producer
Current events show. Magazine format covering news and recreational ideas for kids. National Television Series.

EDUCATION
University of Amsterdam (Dutch), Storefront Actors Theatre / Oregon Shakespearean Festival in Ashland, Oregon (Work Study Program), Sandberg Institute of Broadcasting (Film and TV Production), Volksuniversiteit (Dutch)

TEACHING
Academy of Journalism at Arnhem, Graduate Degree Program. California, Contra Costa School District: High School Program. Mill Valley, California: "Young Filmmaker's Program." Media Training; "Understanding Copyright Law."

TECHNICAL SKILLS
Writing, Editing, Videography, Still Photography, Audio Recording, Nonlinear/Linear Editing, Teaching. Excellent computer skills; Macintosh, OSX, Windows, PC. Movie Magic, Excel, Final Cut Pro, iMovie, Cleaner 5, ProTools, DVD Authoring, Webcasting, Streaming media; Windows Media, Real Media, Real Player, Quicktime Streaming and Progressive. Dreamweaver, HTML. Advanced computer skills.

LANGUAGE SKILLS
Native English, Fluent Dutch, First-Level French.

Social Work Resume Sample: Chronological/Entry Level

Social Work Assistant

Bob Enweive
478 Orwell Way
Jamaica, NY 11445
718-924-4467
bob2000@aol.com

OBJECTIVE:

Obtain an assistant role with a nonprofit social services agency or organization

WORK EXPERIENCE:

December 05 – June 06
Association for the Help of Retarded Children
Assistant Live-in Manager

April 04 – February 05
John Jay College Safety and Security Department
Security Guard

February 02 – June 02
New York State Division of Parole
Intern

May 00 – April 02
Association for Children with Mental Disability
Direct Care Counselor

EDUCATION:

John Jay College of Criminal Justice
Bachelor of Arts, cum laude, February 05

Social Work Resume Sample: Chronological/Entry Level, continued

SKILLS:

Computer/working knowledge of Microsoft Word and Excel
C.P.R. First Aid Certificate 06
AMAP (Approved Medication Administration Personnel) Certified 06
Security Management Certificate 04

HONORS/AWARDS:

Member, John Jay College Honor Roll, 01-05
Member, Chi Alpha Epsilon National Honor Society, 01-05

EXTRACURRICULAR ACTIVITIES:

John Jay College:
> Member, College Alumni Association, 05
> Member, College Students for Self-Empowerment Club, 04
> Member, College President Search Committee, 03-04

Social Work Resume Sample: Chronological/Individual Contributor

SOCIAL WORKER, HEALTH AND HUMAN SERVICES

STAN DUPPE
7 LARK COURT
NEW HYDE PARK, NY 11040
516-672-3959
S.DUPPE@YAHOO.COM

SUMMARY OF QUALIFICATIONS

- Three years of Social Work experience and solid understanding of functional areas and practices
- Four-plus years of Administrative Assistant and Customer Service experience

WORK EXPERIENCE

June 2006 – December 2006
Health and Human Services Office, Belleville, New York
Social Work Analyst
- Produce a variety of customized reports on various client demographics using advanced MS Office skills, including Excel, Access, and Word
- Use SQL, Excel, and other tools to maintain and analyze data and identify data issues
- Assist with system maintenance and administration

August 2005 – June 2006
Department of Welfare Services, Garden City, New York
Welfare Services Coordinator
- Assisting Manager to reorganize and develop the Resource Department which includes three locations regionally and covers a population of 150 clients with multiple welfare needs
- Enrollment, tracking, and termination of all benefits
- Research new benefit programs in effort to keep benefits for clients equally
- Client communications and special event planning
- Monitor agency wide online computer and job training
- Handle various requests from agency (New York State Department of Labor, Social Security, etc.)
- Designed job section of agency intranet and manage weekly updating using MS Front Page

Social Work Resume Sample: Chronological/Individual Contributor, continued

January 2003 – January 2005
Casual Credit Corporation, Bronx, New York
Human Resources Assistant
- Assist human resources with all recruiting functions, including job posting, resume screening, interview scheduling, and conducting interviews and reference checks
- Relieve human resources of all clerical work and minor administrative and business detail
- Conduct new hire orientation and process all new hire and benefits paperwork
- Aid current employees with any and all human resource related issues and process all employee status changes
- Backup payroll department
- Arrange companywide social events and travel
- Client services professional
- Responsible for researching and resolving complaints to ensure customer retention and satisfaction
- Provided account information and consumer credit counseling program status and updated files
- Daily communication with banking institutions to ensure effectiveness of consumer credit counseling program

EDUCATION

May 2004
Hilltop College, Patchogue, New York
Bachelor's Degree - Business Administration - Management

COMPUTER SKILLS

- Skilled user of Microsoft programs such as Word, Excel, Access, Outlook, Lotus Notes, ACT, Front Page, Publisher, and PowerPoint
- Data entry and keyboarding skills of 60 wpm

Social Work Resume Sample: Functional/Senior Manager

SENIOR SOCIAL WORK MANAGER

Nan Proffette
699 E. 23rd St.
Brooklyn, NY 11218
718-434-8974
n.proffette@gmail.com

Summary Profile

Social Work/Network Development Consultant and Manager with proven initiative and skills in strategic planning, development, management, and training. Broad spectrum of industry experience includes publishing, human resources, economic development, and non-profit development. Record of outstanding achievement in enhancing visibility and expanding market scope. Areas of expertise include:

- Coalition Building/Network Development
- Feasibility Studies/Needs Assessments
- Ethnic/Target Marketing

Employment

- Conducted feasibility study for the Brooklyn Collaborative, a coalition of minority organizations in South Brooklyn (St. Nicholas Neighborhood Preservation Corps, Southside United Housing Development Fund Inc., United Jewish Organizations of Williamsburg, Brooklyn Navy Yard Development Corp.) formed to explore economic development opportunities for their communities. Presented final report to prospective vendors and funding sources, resulting in the initiation of several outsourcing contracts. (1996–1999)

- Established and directed the Occupational Skills Training Institute in Brooklyn, a business school offering paralegal and office skills training. Coordinated licensing effort, curriculum, and site development. Networked with community-based organizations and used advertising campaigns and public presentations to recruit students and staff. Oversaw the design of brochures, catalog, and marketing materials. (1995)

Social Work Resume Sample: Functional/Senior Manager, continued

- Directed the New York City Human Resources Administration / Aid to Dependent Children with Unemployed Parent Work Experience Program for Brooklyn and Queens. Cultivated partnerships with public, private, and nonprofit organizations and negotiated placement agreements. Fostered the development of work experience opportunities for displaced professionals. Developed over 200 host sites and managed worksite relationships. (1992–1994)

- Revitalized a citywide job placement program, sponsored by the Professional Career Services of America, serving displaced middle managers and executives. Researched and developed job leads for applicants, improving quality and range of placement opportunities. Developed ancillary services for applicants including career transition preparation, interview/networking coaching, resume writing, job search support clubs, and skills assessment. Trained placement counselors and support staff, greatly improving the quality of service. (1992)

- Formed a diverse coalition of organizations and community leaders to support efforts of Steven Spielberg's Survivors of the Shoah Visual History Foundation. Implemented a media campaign that successfully recruited survivors and interviewers for the project. (1999–2001)

Education/Certification

New York University, B.A. in Social Science, 1983
New York State Department of Education, Licensed Proprietary Business School Director, 1996

Publication

Priority Publishing, Newburgh, NY, 2005–2006
As Director of Development, successfully launched the subscription and distribution of Social Work Today, its flagship publication:

- Designed, developed, and maintained a proprietary, Microsoft Access database program.

- Monitor subscription activity, facilitate and track subscription mailings.

- Oversee fiscal management by building payments and extracting them to an external online credit card processing application.

- Produce statistical analysis of customer demographics and subscription growth.

- Mine the data for fundraising prospects and leads.

- Facilitate the fulfillment of subscription mailings and streamline the process.

Social Work Resume Sample: Functional/Senior Manager, continued

- Resolve processing issues related to mailing, payments, and delivery.

- Develop independent resources for gaining additional subscribers.

- Manage regular advertising campaigns and public presentations.

- Wrote and edited a series of press releases, oversaw the creation and placement of Web site banner links, e-mail and HTML format conversion, developing other collateral marketing materials such as brochures, posters, and subscription sign-up forms.

- Meet with potential donors, professional advisors, and other key contacts in the community to promote the publication, open new funding channels, and educate our target market.

- Represent magazine at conferences, seminars, donor receptions, and other events

Neighborhood Development

Kensington Community Development, Brooklyn, NY 2004–Present
Director of Development

- Development of a neighborhood prospecting list, compile and edit lists.

- Brochure and solicitation materials development.

- Organize and oversee community events, ongoing mailings, advertising, publicity, and information updates.

- Supervise the recording and processing of funds, receipts, and thank-you letters.

- Meet with the block captains and assist in the individual block fundraising efforts.

- Develop prospective donors & solicit larger donations from outside the community. Oversee fundraising events and meetings.

- Develop volunteer committee and oversee fundraising projects and ideas, using the resources of these volunteers.

Social Work Resume Sample: Chronological/Manager

SOCIAL WORK MANAGER, CHILDREN'S SERVICES

Al Beseeniya
103 Paulson St. #278
Brooklyn Heights, NY 11201
(718) 658-1319
hello7711@comcast.net

OBJECTIVE:

Director of Social Education and Youth Services

EXPERIENCE:

2005 – Present
GREATER NEW YORK SOCIAL CENTER, New York, NY
Director of Education and Youth Services
Assisted in establishing four new community centers focused on serving concentrations of Mexican immigrants in Brooklyn, Queens, the Bronx, and Manhattan.

- Identified new sites.
- Developed systems and policies for day-to-day operations.
- Obtained and complied with all NYC Department of Health licensing for Summer Day Camps and School Age programs.
- Oversaw the implementation of Department of Youth and Community Development "Out of School Time" initiative in the South Bronx center.
- Monitor programs for compliance, accuracy, and accomplishment of objectives as required by Robin Hood, Altman, and Pinkerton Foundations.
- Developed "Finding Our Roots" curriculum for all school-age and teen programs.
- Developed contract for Child Adult Center Food meals program serving meals to school-age and Youth-at-Risk population.
- Developed and implemented systems for reporting and evaluating program outcomes.
- Present the agency and its services to school boards, community boards, and other public forums.

Social Work Resume Sample: Chronological/Manager, continued

2002 – 2005
COMMUNITY ASSOCIATION OF PROGRESSIVES, New York, NY
Department Head, Education and Youth Development
- Oversaw and managed 25 educational programs and staff of 100 including Beacons Centers (Department of Youth and Community Development).
- Opened new facility for Day Care center serving two- to five-year-olds and set up Universal Pre K instructions for four-year-olds.
- Set up and organized nine after-school programs.
- Set up and operated an extended-day after-school program model to serve all students in Amber Charter School.
- Expanded programming in United Way funded Community Achievement Project in the Schools Attendance Improvement and Dropout Prevention program, adding three new high schools, serving the Bronx and Manhattan.
- Implemented programming for holiday, summer camps, and TASC (Treatment Accountability for Safer Communities) programs.
- Develop contracts for Child Adult Center Food meals program for 400 participants.
- Develop and implement systems for reporting and evaluating program outcomes.
- Fiscal monitoring of a $2.5 million budgetss contractss and grants.
- Monitor adherence to appropriate policies and procedures to city and government contracts and regulations of Department of Education and Department of Health codes.

2000 – 2002
EAST SIDE YMCA OF GREATER NEW YORK, New York, NY
Branch Supervisor, School-Age Director
Responsible for start-up, staffing development, and expansion of three corporation-funded Virtual Y programs and four school-age programs, one of which was government funded.
- Supervised a staff of 25 and provided ongoing staff development.
- Monitored Agency of Child Development subsidizes and voucher child care programs.
- Maintained all city and government contracts and ensured adherence to the state and city Department of Health codes and guidelines.

1998 – 2000
VICTIM SOCIAL SERVICES, Brooklyn, NY
Child Care Supervisor
Responsible for start-up, staffing, and development of programs. Supervised two Child Care Specialists. Developed and managed child care center for drug-exposed infants and children. Organized parent and child activities along with parent training workshops.

Social Work Resume Sample: Chronological/Manager, continued

1996 – 1998
CHILDCARE CUSTODIANS INC., New York, NY
Resource Counselor Specialist
Special assignment from the New York State Office of Mental Health to organize labor manage-
ment meetings regarding needs assessments on child care issues.

EDUCATION:

2006 FEDERATION OF PROTESTANT WELFARE AGENCIES, INC.
Informed Leadership Certificate Program, Orientation Series, New Board Members
2002 ROBERT J. MILANO SCHOOL OF MANAGEMENT.
NEW SCHOOL UNIVERSITY GRADUATE SCHOOL, New York, NY
Certificate, Hispanic Leadership Institute, Executive Management Certificate program
1987 NATIONAL UNIVERSITY, Garden City, NY
Certificate courses in Developing Curricula in Substance and Alcohol Abuse
Elementary and Intermediate Grade Levels
1985 COLLEGE OF NEW ROCHELLE, New Rochelle, NY
B.A. in Psychology and Elementary Education

COMMUNITY AFFILIATIONS:

1992-1996 New York City Community Planning Board Three - Youth Services Member
1993-1996 New York City Community School District One - Youth Services Member

INDEX